7/14/16

Weaponizing Information: Propaganda Warfare in the 21ˢᵗ Century

HRISQ
Hampton Roads International Security Quarterly

Vol. XVI (2016) Nr. 1

Transatlantic Euro-American Multimedia LLC
www.teamultimedia.com

Editorial & Subscription Data

Hampton Roads International Security Quarterly (HRISQ) is dedicated to issues effecting the cohesion and vital interests of the Atlantic Community. In recognition of the interconnectivity of the modern world, HRISQ covers direct transatlantic issues as well as functional or geographic "out-of-area" issues relevant to Europe and the United States. Most importantly, HRISQ serves as a forum for both North American and European experts and policy-makers to present their positions to readers on the respective opposite shore of the Atlantic.

Previous focus topics have included: European Security & Defense Initiative; Terrorism and the Atlantic Community; NATO Expansion; Implications of Chinese Expansion for Atlantic Security Interests; Armed Forces Transformation in Europe and the United States; Implications of the Iraq Conflict for US-European Relations.

Hampton Roads International Security Quarterly is published by Transatlantic Euro-American Multimedia LLC, a Virginia-registered limited liability company.

Editor: Sidney E. Dean

SUBSCRIPTIONS:

HRISQ is published in electronic and in print format. Subscriptions can be purchased online through our website www.TEAMultimedia.com, or through a subscription agent. Institutional customers are welcome to submit Purchase Orders. We welcome subscribers from all nations. Our ordering process supports multiple currencies and international fulfillment.

For more information about ordering, please visit our website at:

www.TEAMultimedia.com

Cover image: US Navy information specialists at work. Courtesy US Navy.

Contents

(Dis-)Information Age Warfare: Countering ISIS, Putin & Co.

Sidney E. Dean, Editor

The phrase "hearts and minds" might be relatively new to global politics, but influencing popular opinion – that of your own citizens and allies, that of your adversaries, and that of the neutral world – has always been a vital element of international politics and of warfare. Early evidence can be found in Egyptian reliefs touting the invincibility of the pharaoh, who was depicted larger than life and surrounded by fallen foes. The message was simple, but clear: Egyptians should support their ruler who defended and brought glory to their nation, while foreigners should submit to his will rather than risk destruction.

Propaganda warfare became more sophisticated over time. During the Cold War the Soviet Union dedicated a huge apparatus to so-called "agitational propaganda" or "AGITPROP". The goal was to promote pro-Soviet movements in the Third World while creating sympathy for Soviet aspirations among western populations. The rise of terrorist violence in the second half of the 20th Century was also paralleled by (dis-)information campaigns designed to gain sympathy for the extremists. At the same time western governments did their best to undermine communist regimes and promote democracy, primarily through broadcast media such as the BBC, Deutsche Welle, Radio Liberty/ Radio Free Europe, or Radio Marti. Ironically the free societies faced (and face) greater communications challenges than tyrants and terrorists. The latter's willingness to lie and distort allows them to present more intense arguments which resonate with many people.

The recent revolution in communications technology has taken 21st Century propaganda warfare into a new dimension. It has also leveled the playing field to the point that a small organization or even one skilled communicator can disseminate a message around the world within minutes. The snowball-potential offered by social media means that one film clip or blog post can be re-tweeted, liked, friended and forwarded to millions of people within days. Traditional media outlets tendency to monitor the net further increases the potential exposure for propaganda messages. Unfortunately, the more outrageous, threatening or extreme the message, the more likely it will be viewed.

The internet's potential as a propaganda dissemination tool was quickly recognized by well-organized and funded groups such as al Qaeda and ISIS, groups which have recruited large numbers of technology- and media-savvy specialists who churn out e-zines, blog posts, twitter campaigns, and eye-popping violent videos. Even pop music and video games have become terrorist recruiting tools. Meanwhile Vladimir Putin's nationalist Russia has also revived disinformation as a major foreign policy tool, albeit with a different tack than ISIS et al. While the latter seek to recruit and incite youth, Russia hopes to convince middle-class, educated Europeans and Americans that, "objectively," Putin is pursuing legitimate national aims, even defending Russia and Russians from an aggressive United States or Ukraine. And once western governments are playing catch-up in their struggle to discredit adversarial propaganda.

This volume brings together fifteen subject experts who discuss the phenomenon of (Dis-)Information Age Warfare, analyze the Russian and Islamist propaganda machines, introduce the civilian and military counter-efforts currently conducted by the United States, and propose additional strategies for countering the flow of propaganda. As always, we wish you interesting reading.

Please visit www.teamultimedia.com To find the latest information on our monographs covering security policy, defense technology and armed forces, and military history.

'Unprecedented' Challenge in Countering Adversarial Propaganda

Lisa Ferdinando

Lisa Ferdinando is a public affairs officer with DoD News.

The United States is facing an unprecedented challenge in countering the propaganda of adversaries who recruit and easily spread misinformation through the Internet, a top defense official told a House panel on October 22, 2015.. While there are many benefits to being in a cyber-connected world, there is also a "dark side" that adversaries are taking advantage of, according to Michael D. Lumpkin, the assistant secretary of defense for special operations and low-intensity conflict. "The scope of our current challenge in the informational space is unprecedented," Lumpkin told the House Armed Services Emerging Threats and Capabilities Subcommittee. Joining Lumpkin at the hearing were Army Major General Christopher K. Haas, director of the force management and development directorate for U.S. Special Operations Command, and Air Force Brigadier General Charles Moore, deputy director for global operations on the Joint Staff.

Immediacy, Wide Reach of Social Media

 The military has a critical role to play in countering adversarial messages, Lumpkin said, noting it is a contributor of unique capabilities and a partner to the whole-of-government effort led by the State Department. The U.S. Special Operations Command's Military Information Support Operations, or MISO, force provides a critical capability in supporting the needs of the military and the overall strategic messaging effort of the State Department, Lumpkin said. "The rise of [the Islamic State of Iraq and the Levant] and the ability for other state and non-state actors to conduct recruitment operations and spread propaganda almost certainly and with minimal cost highlights the dark side, one that requires the whole-of-government response."

Unlike television or radio broadcasts, social media and other Internet communications allow for interactive discussions "anytime and in almost any location with virtually unlimited reach," Lumpkin emphasized. "Social media and other communications technologies have enabled the virtual and, in some cases, actual mobilization of dispersed and demographically varied audiences around the world." The communications allow non-state actors to "reach across the globe with multiple, simultaneously targeted and tailored approaches to motivate or manipulate a spectrum of audiences," he said.

Limitless Reach

 Preparing the MISO forces for current and future conflict is an important role for the U.S. Special Operations Command, Haas said. Citing what he described as the "extensive propaganda efforts employed by both ISIL and Russia," Haas said the role of the U.S. Special Operations Command in manning, training and equipping is especially critical. While significant improvements have been made over the last decade, challenges remain, he said.

To address capability gaps, U.S. Special Operations Command is developing a plan to expand MISO training into social media use, online advertising, web design and other areas, he explained.

Global Military Information Efforts

MISO forces are currently deployed to 21 U.S. embassies, working with country teams and interagency partners to challenge adversary information and support broader U.S. government goals, Moore said. The military information forces use existing web and social media platforms such as Facebook, Twitter and YouTube to support military objectives by shaping perceptions while highlighting ISIL atrocities, coalition responses to ISIL activities, and coalition successes. MISO personnel have the training and cultural understanding to assess enemy propaganda activities and propose unique solutions that support U.S. military objectives, he explained.

Moore said MISO efforts in the Central Command area of responsibility are focused on challenging violent extremists. In the European Command's area of responsibility, he said, the efforts of military information forces include "exposing Russian mistruths and their concerted efforts to mislead European audiences as to their true intentions."

Also at the hearing was Matthew Armstrong of the Broadcasting Board of Governors, the independent federal entity that oversees government broadcasting including the Voice of America. Moore said European Command is looking to expand its engagement with the Broadcasting Board of Governors to further improve information dissemination capabilities.

Confronting Putin's Hybrid Wars in an Engagement Age

Maksymilian Czuperski

Maksymilian Czuperski is special assistant to the president of the Atlantic Council in Washington DC. He presented this analysis as expert testimony before the US Senate Committee on Foreign Relations Subcommittee on Europe & Regional Security Cooperation on November 3, 2015.

Chairman Johnson, Ranking Member Shaheen, Members of the Committee, I am honored to appear before you today. As a Polish citizen, I was raised on a continent that was defined by the vision of a Europe whole, free, and at peace. A Europe in which the children of those who were once enemies became each other's best friends, and in which freedom, democracy, and tolerance have served as unifying forces during the longest era of peace and prosperity on the European continent. A Europe in which diversity laid the foundation not for bloodshed and violence, but solidarity and progress. This Europe has become a beacon of hope—an opportunity for a better future for the thousands who risk their lives as they seek to reach its shores, or remain steadfast in the face of oppression and injustice, just to inch closer to that dream.

But today this vision—which has long been a key US strategic goal—and the continent this vision helped define are being tested by forces that seek to undermine the Europe I grew up in. No geopolitical event has made that more clear than Russia's invasion of Ukraine last year. And, critically, it is not only Russian boots on the ground that challenge the vision of a Europe whole, free and at peace, but also a raging propaganda machine aiming to destroy the West's confidence in its ideals and accomplishments in Europe.

This Russian-led propaganda machine has become so effective that we, as the United States and Europe, have sleep-walked into the unimaginable: the armed annexation by one state of territory belonging to another, an act not seen in Europe since 1945. This propaganda machine is providing cover for a revisionist Russian leader to reverse the progress that the Western nations have made together in Europe over the past two decades, and create a Europe divided, dictated to, and at war.

"I can tell you outright and unequivocally that there are no Russian troops in Ukraine."[1] – These were the words of Vladimir Putin, and they were, outright and unequivocally, a lie.

---

[1] http://en.kremlin.ru/events/president/news/49261

In fact, Putin has been lying to his own people while Russian citizens and soldiers have been fighting and dying in a war of his own making. Thanks to the propaganda machine he has built; it has been possible for the Kremlin to deny any allegations of Russian involvement in Ukraine. Said Foreign Minister Sergei Lavrov in January of this year: "If you allege [that Russian troops are in Ukraine] so confidently, present the facts. But nobody can present the facts, or doesn't want to. So before demanding from us that we stop doing something, please present proof that we have done it."[2]

When Western officials did indeed present strong evidence that Russian troops have been deployed in Ukraine, the Kremlin was quick to dismiss the evidence as "just images from computer games"[3] and has sought to discredit information released by NATO, the US government, and its European allies as a "smear campaign."[4] And for a long time the Kremlin succeeded, because today's information systems are also, unfortunately, hotlines through which ill-intentioned leaders can channel misinformation.

As we stumbled while Europe's borders were redrawn, a broader new reality was also emerging: We are no longer merely in an information age, in which narratives are shaped by one flow of information pushing against another and simply presenting the truth can discredit lies. Today, we are in **the engagement age** whereby the narratives we create are shaped by how we communicate with one another. Unlike the past, we have unprecedented power to access vast amounts of information that is now in citizens' hands, not to mention the power to create, engage with, share and most importantly discover this information freely. It is a new age that has brought the world and Europe itself closer together, and made it more open, but that is now being hijacked by less benevolent forces such as those of Mr. Putin.

Moscow has seized this new space through a concentrated and engaging propaganda campaign— hybrid information warfare if you will—with the aim of sowing confusion and encouraging or justifying the West's ambivalent response to Russia's aggression, now also in Syria.

Troll-shops and cutting-edge media factories in Russia work around the clock to engage and misinform their audience through flashy content. We know this, because all of us have seen the deceptive videos posted online by the outlet RT that today claims to be the most watched news network on YouTube with over 2 billion views.[5] And some of those who were tasked with the job of spreading lies 140 characters at a time, such as 34-year-old Lyudmila Savchuk, have come out providing us with a rare glimpse into what happens within these shops.[6]

This spreading of "digital breadcrumbs" is an attempt to undermine our Western narrative and values, and divide NATO and the EU, by exploiting divisions within both nations and communities.

But the engagement age has also reached Russia. In fact, the Kremlin has recognized the potential of this new age to the degree that it is concerned about its impact on its own people. Several weeks before Mr. Putin sent his troops—little green men as they were known—to Crimea and launched his propaganda assault on Ukraine, he first struck at home:

[2] http://www.reuters.com/article/2015/01/22/us-ukraine-crisis-davos-poroshenko-idUSKBN0KU1TX20150122
[3] http://www.nbcnews.com/storyline/ukraine-crisis/kremlin-satellite-images-russian-troops-computer-games-n191771
[4] http://www.bbc.com/news/world-europe-28492474
[5] https://www.rt.com/news/214723-rt-two-billion-youtube/
[6] http://www.voanews.com/content/russians-get-glimpse-of-internet-troll-factory/2846484.html

On January 24, 2014 the Russian equivalent of Facebook, the network VKontakte, with its 60 million daily users, was forcefully taken over from its former CEO Pavel Durov, by businessmen allied with Mr. Putin in an attempt to control the potential dangers of the engagement age to Russia's leadership.

But, while Mr. Putin is attempting to control the digital space, there are limits to the level of control that can be put on opportunities for the Russian people to engage with one another and to discuss what is actually happening in Russia.

This also provides us with new opportunities to challenge Mr. Putin's propaganda machine.

The desire to share and connect is a fundamental value shared by all. Hence, rather than rely on government information to expose Mr. Putin's lies, the Atlantic Council's report, 'Hiding in Plain Sight: Putin's War in Ukraine', collected and presented the facts that the Kremlin had been trying to hide by tapping into people's desire to share and engage: When we post selfies, videos, photos, tweets, and Facebook updates then we frequently leave so called "digital breadcrumbs" behind that are often publicly accessible and even entail geotags with the exact geographical details of where a crumb was created. Anyone can access these "digital breadcrumbs." But we of course don't take these face value, which why using innovative digital forensic research and verification techniques including geolocating we can differentiate between fact and fiction. This allowed us tell the true story of Russia's war in Ukraine.

This was no civil war. The evidence presented in 'Hiding in Plain Sight' makes clear that the conflict in Ukraine's east is a Kremlin-manufactured war, fueled by Russian equipment, fought by Russian soldiers, and directed by Mr. Putin.

Our team at the Atlantic Council was able to reveal numerous cases of Russian soldiers being sent to fight in Ukraine. One of them was Bato Dambayev of the 37th Motorized Infantry Brigade who, after participating in the fierce fighting in Donbas, returned home to the city of Buryita along the Russian-Mongolian border more than 4000 miles from the Ukrainian conflict. An ordinary Russian soldier, he had trained at large camp near the Russian city of Kuzminka from where he was sent across the border to fight in Ukraine. Like many of his friends, he documented his adventure by posting selfies and pictures along the way.

For a long time, the Kremlin has succeeded in setting the narrative for the Ukraine conflict, even managing to convince many that it is purely a civil war. But the story of Bato and thousands of others like him shows a different reality. The innovative methods used to show Bato's journey, are also the methods our colleague, award winning citizen journalist Eliot Higgins and his team at Bellingcat, used to uncover the Russian military brigade that is believed to have supplied the very BUK missile launcher that downed the civilian aircraft known as flight MH17.

But if we could expose Russia's war in Ukraine despite it being publicly denied by its leader, we asked ourselves, what potential did these methods hold for civil society leaders and journalists?

That's why we shared our findings with Simon Ostrovsky of VICE News. He was able to follow the journey of Bato and verify once again that these innovative digital forensic research methods and open source intelligence produce results. As we watched Simon standing in the very locations that Bato's selfies were taken, we recognized that one of the strongest means of protecting our narrative against misinformation is equipping and training journalists with these new methods, to use in both their own countries and abroad. We also produced this body of research for an even more compelling reason: If the international community cannot distinguish fact from fiction, or chooses not to do so in public, it is unlikely to coalesce around an effective strategy to support Ukraine and deter Mr. Putin.

Our experience taught us that:

1) The best antidote to misinformation in this hybrid war is clarity; to speak the truth but foremost to empower the public to reveal and communicate it clearly
2) Second, social media forensics and geolocation analysis are powerful tools:
   - Information once available only to intelligence agencies is now available to all. We do not need to engage in an information war, rather we need to empower civil society, journalists and citizens to distinguish between fact and fiction.
   - This matters: because it can help overcome the healthy skepticism that the public may have toward official government narratives.
   - This is the new reality of a world in which individuals and non-governmental actors play critical roles in the engagement era.
   - The best part is—you don't need to believe me or my co-authors—the methods we've used in our report are essentially a tool that we don't control.

This is the principle behind the concept of 'information defense' put forward by our colleague Ben Nimmo, a British specialist in analyzing information warfare. He argues that the key to defeating disinformation is to support media, academics and civil society in gathering information on areas of particular concern, so that they can debunk any disinformation as soon as it is released.[7] We therefor recommend expanding that support into the digital arena through concrete training programs and workshops for journalists, civil society leaders, and ordinary citizens, not only here at home but also in regions most effected by the propaganda war, so that they can navigate the engagement age more effectively and do so equipped with groundbreaking new digital forensic research methods.

This concept was proven in Syria, where colleagues such as the Bellingcat group and blogger Ruslan Leviev have spent four years building up an intelligence picture of the conflict from social media.[8] When Russia began bombing targets in Syria and claiming that they were from the Islamic State, it took Ruslan Leviev just hours to prove that the Russians were lying, and were in fact hitting the moderate opposition. Russia's claim that it is focusing on IS was shredded on the first day—leaving it without the diplomatic legitimacy that striking IS would give.

It is important to bear in mind that Mr. Putin has used the Ukrainian and Syrian crises first and foremost to consolidate his own authority at home, whipping up patriotic sentiment to paper over the Kremlin's own failures in governance while repressing civil society, independent media, and social networks.

Chairman Ed Royce rightly pointed out in his Wall Street Journal op-ed earlier this year, that Russia's propaganda machine, "may be more dangerous than any military, because no artillery can stop their lies from spreading and undermining US security interests in Europe"[9]—For that it is time that we put resources where they matter as we did in the

---

[7] http://www.li.com/events/information-at-war-from-china-s-three-warfares-to-nato-s-narratives

[8] https://www.bellingcat.com/news/mena/2015/09/07/are-there-russian-troops-fighting-in-syria/

[9] http://www.wsj.com/articles/countering-putins-information-weapons-of-war-1429052323?alg=y

Cold War, but with the understanding that a new era requires new thinking and new solutions: It is time that we don't blindly push information, but engage in the digital infosphere with our citizens so that they can play a role in distinguishing between fact and fiction. This requires empowering citizens to be part of the process and stopping those who otherwise attempt to blind.

Therefore, revealing Putin's deception of his own people is a key part of a strategy to end his aggression in Europe, by hitting him where he is vulnerable.

We must also demonstrate solidarity with those Russians who are courageous enough to take a stand against the lies of the Putin regime.

The first victims of Putin are the people of Russia, who deserve better.

Confronting Mr. Putin's aggression does not imply a confrontation against the Russian people. As the co-signers of the preface in our report 'Hiding in Plain Sight' point out: "We all share a common vision for a Europe whole, free, and at peace, in which Russia finds its peaceful place. But Mr. Putin's war in Ukraine threatens this vision and the international order."[10]

---

[10] http://www.atlanticcouncil.org/publications/reports/hiding-in-plain-sight-putin-s-war-in-ukraine-and-boris-nemtsov-s-putin-war

A Transatlantic Strategy for Ukraine: Countering Russia and Driving Reform

Vladimir Putin's invasion of the Crimea and deployment of armed forces to eastern Ukraine requires a determined and strong response from the United States and from Europe, acting jointly through NATO and the European Union.

In this volume, eleven policy experts and policy makers discuss the Transatlantic options for containing further Russian aggression, to protect the Ukraine and to deter Russian threats toward other European nations. European, American and joint Transatlantic policy responses are considered, but the emphasis is on United States actions, as the USA is the only NATO partner with sufficient military power to back up diplomatic and political initiatives with a credible threat of consequences.

To order please visit www.teamultimedia.com

Russian Propaganda: Ways and Means

Leon Aron

Dr. Leon Aron is Resident Scholar and Director of Russian Studies at the American Enterprise Institute. He presented this analysis as expert testimony before the Senate Foreign Relations Committee, Subcommittee on Europe and Regional Security Cooperation, on November 3, 2015.

First, a disclaimer: the testimony I am about to give will be given in my capacity as a private expert and not as a Governor of the Broadcasting Board of Governors.

The aggressive, often sophisticated and Internet-savvy propaganda campaign, underwritten by the Russian government to the tune of at least half a billion dollars a year, is flexible and skillfully adapted to the geography of the audience. While general patterns are similar and I will discuss them in a moment, content may differ considerably depending on the ethnicity, political culture and geography of the intended audience.

Thus, in Western Europe and the United States, the RT television network aims not so much to "sell" what might be called the "Russia brand," but rather to devalue the notions of democratic transparency and accountability, to undermine confidence in objective reporting, and to litter the news with half- truths and quarter truths.

"Question more!" is RT's advertising motto – and it is not coincidental. For the Russian network seeks to exploit several key conventions and tendencies of Western media:

> ***First**, truth is in the eye of the beholder. As a keen and formerly inside observer of the Russian media effort put it, Russian propaganda uses "the idea of a plurality of truths to feed disinformation, which in the end looks to trash the information space."[1]
> * **Second**, that there are two sides to every story, and the credibility of the source is secondary.

"The medium is the message," Marshall McLuhan famously proclaimed in the 1960s. Half a century later, the message is increasingly detached from the medium, and words from those who utter them. After all, post-modernism postulates that "there is no author, there is only the text." My favorite modern English poet, Robert Graves, started the poem, titled "Forbidden Words," with these four lines:

"There are some words [that] carry a curse with
them: Smooth-trodden, abstract, slippery vocables.
They beckon like a path of stepping stones;
But lift them up and watch what writhes or
scurries!"

But when showered by these smooth-trodden and slippery vocables, how often do Western media bother to lift the stones?

> ***Third**: since the credibility of the source is of secondary importance, Russian propaganda finds itself fitting rather smoothly into a panoply of Western media. (Just to be on the safe side, RT, which does not broadcast in Russian, never identifies itself as a Russia-based and government-funded network.)

---

[1] Stephen Castle, "A Russian TV Insider Describes a Modern Propaganda Machine," *New York Times,* February 13, 2015.

* **Fourth**: RT and the Sputnik news network, launched last year, find the soil of the Western media markets already fairly loosened and fertilized as far as conspiracy theories are concerned. Did the US government orchestrate 9/11? Why not? 23 percent

   of Germans thought so, as did 15 percent of Italians.[2] Seven years after the fall of the Twin Towers, between a quarter and one-fifth of Britons, French and Italians told the pollsters they had no idea who was behind the attack.[3] Well, then, after the CEO of

   France's largest oil company, Total, who had opposed economic sanctions on Russia, was killed when his plane slammed into a snowplow operated by a drunken driver at a Moscow airport, Russian commentators asserted that he was killed by the CIA. [4] And why stop there? Did the CIA aid Ukrainians in shooting down the MH 17 Malaysian airliner (one of the "versions" suggested by Russian propaganda)? Plausible. Did the Russian opposition kill its own leader, Boris Nemtsov, to embarrass Putin? Possible.

* **Fifth:** With all the so-called value judgments to be taken out of the reporting, there are no more "just" wars or wars of "aggression" -- only "conflicts." Just as there are no "victims" and "perpetrators," only "violence." So when RT and Sputnik editors read or see or hear news in the leading Western media about "renewed violence" in the "conflict" between Ukraine and Russia, they find it easy to build up on and extrapolate from them to twist the truth. Especially, when almost one in three Germans was reported last summer to find Russia not responsible for the violence in Ukraine, that's another opening for RT to exploit.
   *

Yet for all this seemingly fertile soil for Russia's distortions, the impact of the Russian disinformation campaign on the democracies of Western and Central Europe appears paltry, if not to say negligible. Where the ratings were credibly established, RT was barely visible, apart from the "pre-sold" audiences on the extreme left and right.[5] The main reason is a highly competitive media environment that exposes people to a wide range of facts and interpretations.

The situation is quite different when we go east, to the countries collectively known as the Former Soviet Union. There the effectiveness of Russian propaganda is greatly enhanced by two factors.

---

[2]   "International Poll: No Consensus on Who Was Behind 9/11." World Public Opinion, September 10, 2008.

[3] Ibid.

[4] Alan Cullison, "Russia Uses MH17 Crash for Propaganda," *Wall Street Journal,* July 23, 2015.

[5] The Daily Beast reports that in 2012, RT's daily viewership did not reach the minimum Nielsen rating threshold of 30,000 people in the United States, and that in Europe, its audience has amounted to less than 0.1 percent of total viewership, except in Britain where it does slightly better, garnering 0.17 percent of the total viewing population in 2015. RT's oft-cited figure of "630 million people in 100 countries" refers to the potential geographical reach of its programming based on where RT is available—not on how many people are actually viewing it.

See: Katie Zavadski, "Putin's Propaganda TV Lies about its Popularity," *The Daily Beast*, September 17, 2015.

First, the presence of ethnic Russian minorities, some of whom nurture grievances; and, second, the existence of far fewer alternative sources of credible information than in West-Central Europe.

It is here that what is known as the "weaponization of information" occurs: news and analysis as a means of provoking strong negative emotions, potentially leading to hatred, incitement and, ultimately, the justification of violence.

A couple of months ago, while searching Russian-language sites for information on the growing presence of Russian fighters with ISIS in Syria, I was directed by one of the links to one of Russia's most popular sites, an equivalent of Facebook called VKontakte, which has hundreds of thousands of visitors each day both from Russia and the Former Soviet Union. Before I could get to the articles I was looking for, I saw pictured at the top of the opening page a cartoonish Uncle Sam holding on his lap a baby clad in a black uniform with a Kalashnikov on its back. The caption read: "ISIS is a project of America's two- party system."

As an expert on Russian propaganda in Estonia put it, this effort has produced "a separate reality created by Russian media" in which he claims many ethnic Russian Estonians already live and which creates enormous problems for democratic politics.

In Kyiv earlier this year one of my most memorable meetings was with the Dean of the School of Journalism at the Kyiv-Mohila Academy, Professor Evhen Fedchenko. Together with his students he runs a website called *StopFake.org*, which records some of the Russian propaganda masquerading as news. Here are a few examples:

- A report in the Russian media that the U.S. President has extended a decree that bans balalaikas (which are traditional Russian musical instruments) in the United States until 2020.
- Russia's most widely watched Pervyi Kanal, or First Channel, television network, broadcast an interview with a terrified woman identified as a refugee from the territory controlled by the Ukrainian government. She said she witnessed Ukrainian soldiers publicly executing the wife and son of a pro-Russian separatist. The child was crucified on a bulletin board, while the woman was allegedly dragged behind a tank until she died. The story was proven to be a complete fake.
- Another popular Russian television channel posted on VKontakte and other social media sites an invented conversation between a Ukrainian military commander and a German doctor in which they discuss in detail the harvesting of internal organs, presumably of deceased members of the pro-Russian population caught up in the fighting. The officer is "quoted" as saying that "we would have a great deal of material to work with, thanks to our Western partners."

    Again, bear in mind that Russian television, especially the news programs I just mentioned are viewed by millions of people, especially ethnic Russians and Russian-speakers, outside Russia.

Fortunately, there is an antidote to this poison. It is impossible, of course, to sanitize all of the lies, given the lopsidedness of the manpower, but there is enough of it to deflate the effort considerably.

As usual, the strongest antidote is a rich, diverse, and uncensored democratic media environment. But as such an environment does not yet fully exist in most post-Soviet states, the U.S. international media effort could be of great help.

Despite being barred from domestic outlets in Russia, the online audience of Radio Free Europe/Radio Liberty and Voice of America online has been growing, reaching 4.7 million this summer. In my office last week, a top Russian pro-democracy leader, Vladimir Milov told me that "Radio Liberty is by far the finest and most influential of unofficial sources of political information and analysis in Russia today!" According to independent research, nearly two million Russians are watching RFR/RL's flagship 30- minute nightly news program *Nastoyashchee vremya* or Current Time online every week.

Last year, a nation-wide Gallup survey in Ukraine showed that the size of the VOA audience across all of its media platforms in the Ukrainian and Russian languages had doubled since 2012 to nearly 7 million adults using VOA every week – that is 18 percent of all adults in Ukraine plus nearly 3 million using RFE/RL.

In Kyiv I was repeatedly struck by the deep appreciation by Ukraine's political and media elites of the content provided by Radio Liberty. RFE/RL content is being recognized as superior not just to the Russian propaganda but, to the output of the oligarch-dominated Ukrainian media, which is just as important. As a result, several top Ukrainian television networks competed for the prime time broadcast rights for Current Time.

Mr. Chairman, we are facing a determined and often refined propaganda effort. From the sophisticated exploitation of Western media patterns and vocabulary to outright lies and crude fakes, the goal remains the same: to undermine the people's trust in democratic politics and policies and in free and fair media. As this effort is vital to the maintenance of the present Russian regime, it will be with us for a long time.

Time, and, talent, and risk-taking innovation and yes, money for US international media will continue to be needed to counter it.

Israel: Background and U.S. Relations

Since 1948, successive U.S. Presidents and many Members of Congress have demonstrated a commitment to Israel's security and to maintaining close U.S.-Israel defense, diplomatic, and economic cooperation. U.S. and Israeli leaders have developed close relations based on common perceptions of shared democratic values and religious affinities. U.S. policy makers often seek to determine how events and U.S. policy choices in the Middle East may affect Israel's security, and Congress provides active oversight of executive branch dealings with Israel and other actors in the region. Some analysts criticize what they perceive as U.S. support for Israel without sufficient scrutiny of its actions or their implications for U.S. Interests.

Israel is a leading recipient of U.S. foreign aid and is a frequent purchaser of major U.S. weapons systems. The United States and Israel maintain close security cooperation— predicated on a U.S. commitment and legal requirement to maintain Israel's "qualitative military edge" over other countries in its region. The two countries signed a free trade agreement in 1985, and the United States is Israel's largest trading partner. Israel has many regional security concerns. By criticizing the international interim agreement on Iran's nuclear program that went into effect in January 2014, Prime Minister Netanyahu may seek to give Israel a voice in an ongoing negotiating process in which it does not directly participate. In addition to concerns over Iran, Israel's perceptions of security around its borders have changed since early 2011 as several surrounding Arab countries have experienced political upheaval. Israel has shown particular concern about threats from Hezbollah and other non-state groups in ungoverned or minimally governed areas in Syria, Lebanon, and Egypt's Sinai Peninsula, as well as from Hamas and other Palestinian militants in the Gaza Strip.

Recent exploitation of offshore natural gas raise the prospect of a more energy-independent future. Israel's demographic profile has evolved in a way that appears to be affecting its political orientation, with various leaders vying for the public's support by interweaving ideology with ethnic, religious, socioeconomic, and national security considerations.

To order please visit www.teamultimedia.com

Putin's Invasion of Ukraine and the Propaganda That Threatens Europe

Heather A. Conley

Heather A. Conley is Senior Vice President for Europe, Eurasia and the Arctic Director, Europe Program Center for Strategic and International Studies (CSIS). This analysis was originally presented as expert testimony before the Senate Foreign Relations Committee on November 3, 2015.

Mr. Chairman, and members of the Sub-Committee, thank you for this opportunity to testify today on a subject of great importance concerning Russian influence in Europe. This is a subject area where there is little holistic understanding of the Kremlin's tools and methodology in either Europe or the United States. Without understanding how this influence works and the various tools that are deployed, we cannot identify appropriate responses to counter and ultimately combat this increasingly effective form of manipulation.

Strategic communications, directed toward both the Russian people and the international community, is an essential part of Russia's full spectrum tool kit designed to shape the 21st century battlespace. There are conventional and non-convention components to this strategy with the conventional or military applications being the most straightforward. Today, Russian submarines are closely examining the locations of European undersea fiber optic cables to disrupt all internet and communication lines, military command and control, essential commerce, the functioning of critical infrastructure, and prevent government communication to its population. This summer, a Russian vessel continuously harassed a Swedish research vessel which was laying a new fiber optic cable that connects Sweden to Lithuania, ultimately preventing the Swedish vessel from laying the cable. Ukrainian military forces have repeatedly underscored the effectiveness of Russian military forces in jamming their radar and military communications in combat as well as UAVs operated by the OSCE to monitor the Minsk ceasefire agreements.[1] Clearly, U.S. and NATO forces need to exercise these various scenarios to better prepare for their eventuality.

The focus of this hearing, however, is to gain a better understanding of the Kremlin's use of non-conventional means to shape and influence public opinion and political outcomes in democratic societies. But, make no mistake, these non-conventional means equally shape the future battlespace.

The origins of the Kremlin's policy were developed shortly following the collapse of the Soviet Union and can be found in Russia's Compatriot Policy. This policy established links to the

---

[1] Amb. Daniel B. Baer. "Ongoing Violations of International Law and Defiance of OSCE Principles and Commitments by Russian Federation in Ukraine." U.S. Mission to the OSCE. October 15, 2015. http://osce.usmission.gov/oct_15_15_ukraine.html

estimated 40 million ethnic Russians and Russian speakers living beyond the newly formed borders of the Russian Federation.[2] The definition of a Russian compatriot has been refined over time but generally a compatriot demonstrates a connection to Russian culture, history, values, and language. More recently, the policy has evolved to justify the protection of ethnic Russians living in the post-Soviet space which means that Russia will intervene in a foreign country's internal affairs on behalf of "their" ethnic Russian populations. In 2013, President Putin approved Russia's Foreign Policy Concept which provided for a "comprehensive toolkit for achieving foreign policy objectives building on civil society potential, information, cultural and other methods and technologies …"[3] to protect ethnic Russians abroad. On March 18, 2014, this policy was the justification for Russia's illegal annexation of Crimea when President Putin stated "Millions of Russians and Russian-speaking people live in Ukraine and will continue to do so. Russia will always defend their interests…"[4]

It is estimated that the Kremlin spends approximately $100 million annually to fund organizations such as *Russkii Mir*, or Russian World Foundation, which support the implementation of its compatriot policy.[5] *Russkii Mir* provides funds to film makers, civil society organizations and political entities that promote the Russian language, Russian policies in general as well as affirm Russia's historical narrative of the period during and after the Second World War, presenting the Soviet Union as a liberator. It is important to note that although this policy has been in place since the mid-1990s, the policy has been accelerated since the advent of the 'color revolutions' beginning in the 2003-2004 period, administratively streamlined in the Kremlin, and significantly funded. In 2005, the Russian Presidential Administration created a specific Department for Inter- Regional and Cultural Relations with Foreign Countries which was designed to renew influence in the post-Soviet space and prevent color revolutions.

---

[2] Nikolai Rudensky, Russian Minorities in the Newly Independent States: An International Problem in the Domestic Context of Russia Today." National Identity and Ethnicity in Russia and the New States of Eurasia. M.E. Sharpe, Inc. 1994. Pp. 58-60

[3] Foreign Policy Concept (2013): Kontseptsiia vneshnei politiki Rossiiskoi Federatsii, http://www.mid.ru/bdomp/Brp_4.nsf/arh/6D84DDEDEDBF7DA644257B160051BF7F?OpenDocument

[4] Vladimir Putin, "Address by President of the Russian Federation." The Kremlin, Moscow. March 18, 2014. http://en.kremlin.ru/events/president/news/20603

[5] Sanita Jemberga, Mikk Salu, Eesti Ekspress, Šarūnas Černiauskas, Dovidas Pancerovas, "The Kremlin's Millions," Re: Baltica. August 27, 2015. http://www.rebaltica.lv/en/investigations/money_from_russia/a/1257/kremlins_millions.html

In 2011, the CSIS Europe Program conducted a comprehensive assessment of the effectiveness of Russia's compatriot policy in Estonia. I ask that a copy of this report be submitted for the record (http://csis.org/files/publication/110826_Conley_RussianSoftPower_Web.pdf). Although the compatriot policy is deployed differently in each country depending on the composition of the population and historical relationship with Moscow, there are common traits.   In Latvia, for example, the *Russkii Mir* Foundation reports that there are approximately 100 Russian compatriot organizations.[6] Increasingly, these compatriot organizations support political parties and individual politicians sympathetic to the Kremlin whose goal is to create an internal political forces within the country to increase Russia's political influence while simultaneously eroding confidence in the democratic state. In Latvia, these organization promote the message that Riga discriminates against its 26% ethnic Russian population by suppressing use of the Russian language and citizenship as well as endorsing neo-fascist political tendencies.

In 2012, these political forces, aided by Russian-owned media outlets, were able to advance a referendum to constitutionally mandate that Russian become the second official language in Latvia (which is currently not allowed by the Latvian Constitution). The referendum was unsuccessful – the Russian language is freely used in Latvia – yet it demonstrated that these well-funded groups, utilizing democratic processes (that are ironically unavailable in an authoritarian Russia) are very capable of internally pursuing the Kremlin's policy agenda, sowing societal divisions and de-legitimizing democratic governments.

These divisive political messages are successfully amplified and magnified through Russian media outlets. Russian news outlets copy their Western media counterparts assiduously, while inserting their own biased commentary into their programming. While they play popular music and cover human interest stories, they also report frequently on rampant corruption and decadence in the West, play on the fears of extremism and non-traditional society, and air "news" stories of fascists taking over in Ukraine and European leaders subservient to their U.S. masters.

But Russian-based networks are not the only channels broadcasting such programming; many of Europe's "independent" news outlets have been purchased by local oligarchs who are in collusion with the Kremlin. Once again, looking to Latvia as an example, the three most popular television

---

[6] See Catalogue, Russkii mir Foundation, http://www.russkiymir.ru/russkiymir/en/catalogue/

stations – which operate commercially -- are either indirectly or directly controlled by the Russian government. Bank Rossiya (which has already been sanctioned by the United States, with $572 million frozen in U.S. accounts)[7] owns half the shares in one station while the other the channels are owned by a single holding company, Baltic Media Alliance (BMA), which has 11 subsidiaries in the Baltic States alone. BMA operates the most popular Russian televisions channel in the Baltic States and rebroadcasts popular Russian television shows. One channel is owned by two Russian oligarchs.[8] Two other Russian television channels are registered in the United Kingdom, hold a UK broadcast license, and fall under British regulatory scrutiny. These television stations were used extensively to encourage signatures for the Russian language referendum in Latvia which prompted the UK regulator to state that the channels had violated British regulations.

Other European countries, such as Bulgaria, also have a very high percentage of Russian owned media outlets which are used effectively to counter government policies, such as anti-corruption or judicial reform as well as policies which support the U.S. or the European Union. In 2012, for instance, VTB Capital - the investment arm of Russia's second largest bank - led a consortium with Bulgaria's Corporate Commercial Bank (KTB) to purchase the largest telecommunications company in Bulgaria, BTC. VTB is 60 percent owned by the Russian government and owns 9 percent of KTB (which also happened to be one of the banks implicated in Bulgaria's summer 2014 banking crisis). Since making these strategic acquisitions, Russia has been accused of using Bulgarian media outlets to advance its national interests. A €20 million media campaign backed widespread anti-shale protests throughout the country, and was handled by several media companies with Russian connections – presumably to keep Bulgaria dependent on Russian oil and gas. These acquisitions have also coincided with a decline in Bulgaria's media independence ranking as tracked by international watch dogs and monitors, including the World Bank and Freedom House.

While Russia's compatriot policy is designed for (and is most efficacious in) former Soviet and Warsaw Pact countries, Western European countries as well as the U.S. are not immune from its

---

[7] Philip Shiskin, "U.S. Sanctions Over Ukraine Hit Two Russian Banks Hardest." *Wall Street Journal*. March 5, 2015. http://www.wsj.com/articles/u-s-sanctions-over-ukraine-hit-two-russian-banks-hardest-1425597150?alg=y
[8] Springe I., Benfelde S., Miks Salu M, (2012): The Unknown Oligarch, *Re: Baltica*, http://www.rebaltica.lv/en/investigations/money_from_russia/a/686/the_unkown_oligarch.html

influence, particularly political party financing in Europe and its pervasive media. In June 2015, a new faction was created in the European Parliament called the "Europe of Nations and Freedoms (ENF)" party. Although newly formed, the ENF consists of 39 members from eight European countries and is unabashedly pro-Kremlin in its positions. As of August 2015, ENF members had voted 93 percent of the time in favor of the Kremlin's positions,[9] and they have opposed the EU's Association Agreement with Ukraine, backed Russia's annexation of Crimea, and refused to condemn the murder of Russian opposition leader, Boris Nemtsov. This new grouping is led by the leader of France's far-right Front Nationale, Marine Le Pen, who received a € million loan from the Moscow-based First Czech-Russian Bank last November.[10]

These pro-Russian EU politicians have been bolstered by Russia's effective and broad-reaching media campaign which has used television, radio, and internet sites as mediums to convey its messages across Europe. The main perpetrator of these tactics is the increasingly sophisticated Russian news outlet, RT (formerly Russia Today). RT purports to reach over 700 million people and has an annual budget comparable in size to the BBC's World News Service. The United Kingdom's media regulator, Ofcom, has recently sanctioned RT for biased coverage of events in Ukraine.

Other effective channels of Russian influence are the Russian Orthodox Church and the use (or, more accurately, misuse) of history propaganda. The compatriot policy also defends and disseminates Russian traditional values, particularly those clash of values between a traditional society and secular democracy, through the voice of the church. Perhaps most insidious is the use of the Soviet historical narrative which portrays the USSR as a liberating power during the Second World War and vanquisher of the Nazis; but not as an occupying power that the West never recognized - a frequent theme on Russian television. Thus, Russian television channels regularly show film documentaries that exhort Russia's liberation and heroic role which continues to reinforce this narrative among ethnic Russian populations. The Russian security services provide

---

[9] Peter Kreko, Marie Macaulay, Csaba Molnar, Lorant Gyori. "Europe's New Pro-Putin Coalition: The Parties of No." Institute of Modern Russia. August 3, 2015. http://imrussia.org/en/analysis/world/2368-europes-new-pro-putin-coalition-the-parties-of-no

[10] Suzanne Faley and Maia de la Baume, "French Far Right Gets Helping Hand with Russian Loan." *The New York Times*. December 1, 2014. http://www.nytimes.com/2014/12/02/world/europe/french-far-right-gets-helping-hand-with-russian-loan-.html?_r=0

substantial funds for the production of such patriotic films. However, native populations in many European countries see the role of the Soviet Union during and after the Second World War quite differently and therefore view these recitations as a diminishment of their own history of independence.

This is the challenge we face and let me be clear, the challenge is daunting. Russia's network of influence has been active for over two decades; it is well funded; and has largely succeeded in creating dense and opaque networks in many NATO countries. These intertwined networks work together to subvert government action, influence policy action, finance political parties and significantly control domestic and international media space. We must educate European and Americans citizens about the Kremlin's true objectives rather than simply hope, as we do today, that they will not be persuaded.

Recognizing the challenge and educating about the nature of the threat is the first step; now the United States and Europe must take effective counter-measures.

I do not believe financing a major U.S.-backed information dissemination campaign toward Russia will be effective. The Kremlin has efficiently closed all access to any independent journalism or media by implementing extraordinary measures to suppress alternative narratives to its prevailing views at the time. In this environment, a State Department fact sheet, no matter how correct, will do very little. However, social networks in Russia do continue to exist that can circumvent these measures to receive independent information through social media. I would urge RFE/RL to explore how to reach and expand these loose social networks but realistically, this will only target a small, urban population and not effect change in Russia.

The United States and Europe must also significantly enhance measures of transparency and diversify the media outlets functioning in our own countries. Countries should insist on greater transparency requirements to identify the true ownership of media holding companies. If one country or its affiliated commercial enterprises acquire an excessively large holding in any one company, efforts should be made to diversify outlets. Television and radio remain the most powerful sources of information in some of the most vulnerable NATO countries. Regulatory mechanisms should be strengthened to control overly-biased coverage, and firm penalties - such as the suspension of broadcasting licenses - should be considered as a deterrent.

Most importantly, the U.S. should also initiate a major anti-corruption/anti-kleptocracy initiative, in cooperation with the European Union, to root out malignant Russian economic influence in Europe. America's greatest soft power instruments are its global fight against corruption and ability to prevent the use or misuse of the U.S. financial system to further corrupt practices. This is the Kremlin's greatest vulnerability and the U.S. has the reach and ability to affect change.

Sadly, when European governments begin to take decisions to suspend media outlets, the Kremlin will cry foul that "free speech" and "media freedoms" have been trampled. If a European government initiates anti-corruption activities, seeks energy independence, or implements banking and judicial reform, media outlets and previously unknown NGOs actively and vociferously work against any reform efforts to enhance transparency. It is perhaps the greatest irony that the Kremlin proactively uses our democratic institutions, civil society and laws to undermine our democracy and erode confidence in our societies. In other words, we can speak exhaustively about Russia's media methods and influence but this is really about how we – the United States and Europe — can strengthen the rule of law and transparency and improve the health in our democracies to fight against this influence. It is our vigilance and our transparency that is needed the most.

Countering Russia's Propaganda Machine

Peter Pomerantsev

Peter Pomerantsev is a Senior Fellow at the Legatum Institute, London, and co-author of a project on countering Russian propaganda in Europe.

The West is belatedly waking up to the power of the Kremlin's media machine. The Supreme Commander of NATO called the annexation of Crimea 'the most amazing information warfare blitzkrieg we have ever seen.' Zhanna Nemtsova, daughter of murdered Russian opposition politician Boris Nemtsov, blames the climate of hate created by Kremlin propaganda for the murder of her father and starting the war in Ukraine. 'We are losing the information war' complains the British head of the House of Commons culture and media committee.

The Soviet Empire may be gone but the Kremlin still has media hegemony over the Russian language space: the 149 million citizens of Russia, as well as the estimated 93 million in the former USSR who have Russian as a fluent first or second language (not to mention a further 5 million or so in Germany).

A recent project by the European Endowment for Democracy, a Brussels foundation, looked for ways to tackle this challenge. I was one of the authors, and we soon found differences between today's situation and the Cold War.

Back in the 20th century the job of Western Russian language media such as the BBC World Service or Radio Free Europe was to break through the information iron curtain. The battle was for alternative points of view and against censorship. Today TV is strictly controlled by the Kremlin inside Russia, but there is easy access to other media online. Meanwhile Russian speakers in Ukraine, Moldova or the Baltics have access to a plethora of media, Kremlin, local and Western, each presenting strikingly contradictory versions of reality.

Take Estonia, where viewers who followed the rival Russian and Western stories of the causes for the downing of MH17 ended up simply disbelieving both sides. Something similar is happening in Kharkiv, a town on the Russian-Ukrainian border, where polls showed a high number of people cynical about all media, whether Russian, Western or Ukrainian. In a landscape where viewers trust no one, they are still most entranced by Russian television channels which, according to Latvian focus group respondents, 'are emotionally attractive, because some news you watch as an exciting movie. You don't trust it, but watch it gladly.'

In order to woo viewers the Kremlin has utterly blurred the lines between fact and fiction. Kremlin 'current affairs' programs are filled with spectacular scare-stories about Russian children crucified by Ukrainian militias or US conspiracies to ethnically cleanse East Ukraine. In a context where no one 'believes' any media, all that matters is that the 'news' is sensationalist and cinematic.

The challenge for independent media is thus not simply to deliver information, but to win trust. This necessitates content that is engaging, reflecting both national and local contexts, and that delves deep into the lived reality of Russian-language speakers across the region.

Reality-based, locally relevant, engaging programming is the one type of content Kremlin media, despite its many successes, does not produce.

News ignores local social problems, whether it's the health service, schools or courts. There is currently no quality Russian language news agency covering the whole of the Russian speaking world. A first step could be to expand the Russian language bureaus of such agencies as the BBC or AFP so they could cover the local news the Kremlin ignores; or create a news-hub that maximized existing sources. One might not be able to convince Kremlin-captive audiences about who shot down MH17, but one can be more relevant to them by focusing on local issues.

Kremlin entertainment meanwhile is largely devoid of socially engaged documentary formats: docu-soaps about institutions such as schools or the army; reality shows exploring ethnic tensions. Local broadcasters need help, both financial and professional, to create this sort of quality content to create the local versions of radio hits like 'This American Life' or 'Make Bradford British', a British documentary program that grappled with ethnic hatred by putting people of different races in one house (in the style of the U.S. show *Big Brother*) and forcing them to confront their prejudices. Imagine a Russian-language program that would use a similar tactic to probe an emotionally charged subject—say, the bitterness between Russians and Ukrainians in a place such as Kharkiv.

New programs could also invite Russians to tackle historical traumas through formats such as the popular BBC series *Who Do You Think You Are?*—a show that follows celebrities as they trace the lives of their ancestors, often engaging with the horrors of twentieth-century wars and genocide. In the Russian case, these kinds of programs would require their subjects to explore the human cost of the gulag, the *holodomor* (Ukraine's enforced famine under Stalin), and the KGB arrests. Some participants would discover their ancestors among the victims; others, among the executioners. In both cases, they would have to reckon with past traumas, a highly emotional and cathartic process. Such content would also allow the audience to move away from the collective historical narratives imposed by the Kremlin, which stress how Russia's leaders, from Stalin to Putin, led the nation to triumph.

Ideally programming would dove-tail with policy priorities: judicial reform in Moldova, for example, accompanied by entertainment shows about courts. BBC Media Action (the charity arm of the BBC funded by grants and not the license fee) have been working with the fledgling Ukrainian public broadcaster on short dramas about young people caught up in the war from different parts of the country. The budget is painfully miniscule but it's exactly the sort of project we need so much more of.

Apart from classical media programmes we should also prioritize media literacy projects which help populations withstand the new Kremlin propaganda and tell the difference between spin and evidence-based inquiry. Online investigative projects, such as Ukraine's myth-busting Stop Fake or Alexey Navalny's corruption-busting website which finds the secret cash stashes of crooked politicians, are powerful not only because of the information they provide, but because they involve citizens in an inter-active, open source search for the truth and thus build communities of trust and critical inquiry.

The key thing is to recognize, as Vladimir Putin understands so well, that media and entertainment are as essential to societies and security as doctors or soldiers. The West made a dreadful mistake in the 1990s, abandoning the development of media in the former Soviet Union to the 'free market': instead media were captured by oligarchs or corrupt regimes, who have used them for malign ends. After the Cold War it was considered part of the 'peace dividend' to slash funding for Radio Free Europe or BBC Russian. A much greater cost is being paid now.

U-Boats "Made in Germany"
German Submarines Today and Tomorrow

By Peter Hauschildt

Since WWI, the terms "German Navy" and "U-Boats" have been virtually synonymous. Non-nuclear submarines remain a mainstay of today's German Navy.

The German shipbuilding industry remains a global technology leader in conventional submarine development. Modern day "U-Boats" are sought after by NATO allies, by Israel, and by other nations around the world. In fact they are a leading export item for Germany's military industry. And the German Navy's U-Boat flotilla is a welcome partner in ongoing NATO and EU security operations.

Some experts believe that German conventional submarines have actually assumed the technological lead over nuclear submarines.

U-Boats "Made in Germany" takes a look at current and future submarine technology being produced or developed in Germany today. Advances in Air Independent Propulsion and Fuel Cell Technology; state-of-the-art Command and Control systems such as the ISUS90 system currently deployed on Class 212A U-Boats; improved sonar, communication suites, and IFF systems; acoustic and electric signature reduction technology; and current as well as developmental weapon systems against underwater, surface, land and aerial targets are all discussed.

The author, Peter Hauschildt, is Director of the Concept Development/R&D Division for German Naval Systems at the leading German ship- and submarine construction firm Thyssen/Krupp Marine Systems / Howaldtswerke Deutsche Werft GmbH (HDW).

U-Boats "Made in Germany": German Submarines Today and Tomorrow is published in cooperation with Marine Forum magazine, and is available exclusively as an e-book. Please click the link on this page to purchase and download from Amazon.com.

To order please visit www.teamultimedia.com

Countering ISIL's Propaganda

Rashad Hussain

Rashad Hussain serves as Special Envoy and Coordinator for Strategic Counterterrorism Communications at the U.S. Department of State. This essay originally appeared on the State Department's DipNote e-zine on 23 November 2015. Reprinted courtesy of U.S. Department of State.

The attacks in Paris, Lebanon, Kenya and Mali have strengthened the deep commitment of the United States to bringing about an end to the violence around the world. These attacks also punctuated the urgency with which we need to continue to work in cooperation with our international partners to counter extremist threats, both in the physical and digital information spaces.

Despite the reality that the vast majority of Muslim communities around the world reject ISIL's propaganda, terrorist groups continue to employ an ideology of brutal violence that exploits various grievances to recruit disaffected youth by offering them a false sense of purpose, belonging, and religious obligation. These groups have been very effective at using the public information space -- particularly social media -- to recruit, radicalize, organize, and promote their ideology. The United States and our partners must operate in the same space and use our technological and innovative strengths to combat the appeal of terrorist groups and to lead the digital fight against extremism.

In this context, the Department's Center for Strategic Counterterrorism Communications (CSCC) has been spearheading an effort to expand partnerships with foreign governments and non-governmental organization partners to directly counter ISIL's messaging, recognizing that other partners around the world will, in some cases, be better positioned to respond to their propaganda.

As a part of this partnership the United States and the United Arab Emirates launched the Sawab Center this past July. The Sawab Center is the first-ever multinational online messaging and engagement program in support of the Global Coalition against Daesh. The Sawab Center uses direct online engagement to counter terrorist propaganda rapidly and effectively, including messages used to recruit foreign fighters, fundraise for illicit activity and intimidate, and terrorize local populations.

The efforts of the Sawab Center have been met with announcements by other governments and organizations to start similar initiatives. For example, in September at the Leaders' Summit on Countering ISIL and Violent Extremism, both the Government of Malaysia and the Organization for Islamic Cooperation to establish similar, regional digital messaging centers.

Nigeria echoed with their own announcement last week and the CSCC will be working in close collaboration with them to establish and expand the network of people willing to speak out against violent extremism. These messaging centers are a part of a network of networks that is connecting governments and civil society, including young people, in an effort to create and amplify positive narratives.

To amplify these positive narratives and respond to the tactics of terrorist groups, we must paint a clear picture of the terror that ISIL creates and the misery that those among them suffer. We must offer a positive vision and alternative paths that allow young people to channel their grievances and talents in productive ways. If terrorists are falsely navigating young people toward a path they call righteous and holy, we must respond by clarifying that the terrorist path is anything but righteous or holy. If Daesh claims to be defending Islam or Muslims, we must illustrate clearly how they are actually destroying Muslim communities. And finally, if terrorists are trying to convince impressionable youths that they will be joining a winning team, we must fight that narrative and convince them that they will be joining a losing one.

As Under Secretary for Public Diplomacy and Public Affairs Richard Stengel noted in an opinion piece in USA Today, "Daesh's brutal methods and intolerant ideology have no place in modern societies and deviate from the teachings of all religious traditions."

We all share a moral responsibility raise our voices both online and in our communities in opposition to Daesh and in support of a more peaceful, prosperous, and brighter future.

Countering Disinformation Through a Free Press

Benjamin Ziff

Benjamin Ziff is Deputy U.S. Assistant Secretary of State. He originally presented this policy review before the Senate Foreign Relations Committee on November 3, 2015

Thank you Chairman Johnson, Ranking Member Shaheen, members of this committee for the opportunity to join you and for the personal investment so many of you have made in our shared vision of a Europe whole, free, and at peace. Your bipartisan support, your visits to Ukraine, the assistance you and your fellow Senators have provided are truly making a difference in the region.

We have all heard popular Kremlin refrains asserting there are no Russian soldiers in Ukraine; that Ukraine is on the verge of collapse; or Americans, and *not corrup leaders*, are the cause of domestic discontent overseas.

While many of these claims can easily be refuted, their around-the clock dissemination attempts to sow doubt, confusion, and suspicion and question even the most basic truths.

The Kremlin sponsors these efforts with a sophisticated $1.4 billion-a-year propaganda apparatus at home and abroad, which claims to reach 600 million people across 130 countries in 30 languages. The Russian government also funds think tanks and outside organizations in its neighboring states to help achieve its goals of promoting the Kremlin's false narratives; portraying the West as a threat; and undermining trust in independent media as well as Western institutions and values.

In the face of the Kremlin's attack on the truth, the free flow of reliable, credible information is the best defense. This is why the State Department has focused its efforts on supporting independent media; improving access to high quality, objective information; exposing false narratives; and building the capacity of civil society. After all, truth should be discovered, not dictated.

Strong independent journalism is a key element in any democracy and will eventually prevail over disinformation and propaganda.

In my remarks today, I will expand upon these areas and describe how we use our public diplomacy tools and foreign assistance to amplify fact-based messages and support credible, independent voices and to improve access to credible information. Finally, I will focus on our diplomatic and security engagements that reinforce the positive story our Allies and partners in Europe tell about our Transatlantic relationship and commitments.

In FY 2015, the State Department and USAID allocated $66 million dollars in U.S. foreign assistance funding to sustain civil society and independent media in the Eurasia and Southeast Europe region, of which more than $16 million supports independent media. In addition to our foreign assistance funds, we have also dedicated $4 million from the public diplomacy budget to bolster our staff and programming. These funds help our partners who are susceptible to Russian aggression build democratic principles, independent media, and a civil society intolerant of corruption.

In FY 2016, President Obama is requesting a 26 percent increase to the State Department and USAID foreign assistance budget in this sector, proposing $83 million to surge our support for civil society and independent media in countries most vulnerable to Russian pressure.

This increase is needed in countries that continue to be under threat of democratic backsliding, especially where the Kremlin's influence is strong and growing—not just in Russian-speaking areas, but also in the Western Balkans. Increasingly, reports indicate that Bosnia and Herzegovina, Serbia, Macedonia and Montenegro are targets of Russian pressure and disinformation. This is not new, but susceptibility is increasing.

We are putting our current public diplomacy and foreign assistance resources to good use, mainly towards programming focused on delivering our messages and supporting local, democratic voices throughout the region.

The Audience

In Western and Central Europe, we work with our European partners to underscore allied unity and bolster resolve to work together on global challenges. We also offer Western journalists opportunities to view the realities on the ground in countries, like Ukraine, where the Kremlin tries to distort the facts.

For Russian-speaking audiences, especially in Eastern Europe and Eurasia, we offer information and programming alternatives while bolstering the capacity of civil society and independent journalists to identify and tackle disinformation. This population is particularly vulnerable to disinformation since Russian is the 10th most-spoken language in the world—the 5th most when counted as a second language — and since ninety percent of all Russian language news, entertainment, and sports in the world are produced in Moscow and controlled by the Kremlin.

Inside Russia, we work with media – traditional and social – to reach the public and maintain a dialogue with the Russian people through programs that accurately describe U.S. policy, society and values. Embassy Moscow is at the forefront of this engagement and has increased its non-governmental exchanges budget by $2 million, and its English language programming by $400,000.

Yet, our work to connect with ordinary Russian citizens continues to be hampered by the Kremlin. All 29 American Corners in Russia were closed down over the last two years, and the Library of Foreign Literature ended our long-standing (22-year) partnership last month, closing the American Center there.

The outcry from ordinary Russians angry about losing this cultural tie with America was immediate and loud. Thanks to them and the efforts of our Embassy team, we relaunched a new American Center on Embassy grounds, and had a huge turnout at its first public event. Our hope is that we can continue to provide an undistorted view of American literature, culture, entertainment, and values to those who seek it in Moscow.

Near-Term: Messaging

On a daily basis, our efforts help audiences identify objective reporting over the Kremlin's noise.

To do this, we employ a combination of short term messaging strategies with medium and long term programs to boost resilience and build capacity to recognize and reject Russian propaganda. The State Department has implemented a rapid response system to support our overseas posts in times of heightened Kremlin propaganda. Armed with the facts, our embassies are able to adapt the content and materials we supply to their own audiences and amplify the truth rapidly.

For example, a few days after the shoot down of the MH17 airliner in July of last year, Embassy Moscow plugged into the State Department's network of 130+ Russian language officers and released hourly messages and content from journalists on the ground to help negate the rampant obfuscation and conspiracy theories being blared by the Russian news media.

Similarly, in September 2015, after photoshopped images alleging U.S. Ambassador Tefft's presence at a Russian opposition rally were released, Embassy Moscow responded by producing a photo collage of the same picture of the ambassador altered to show him at various events - including landing on the moon. The embassy's success in discrediting the risible attempt at propaganda went viral, reaching over one million Russians, and forcing the Russian news outlet that shopped the image to withdraw its own story.

This kind of "rapid response" counter messaging, while necessarily reactive, is crucial to defend against the manipulation of truth. But the best defense against Russian propaganda gaining traction is proactive. It is designed to instill strength and independence in local communities and allies fighting propaganda on the front lines and it encourages higher standards of journalism.

For Ukraine, we are constantly reviewing our policies and needs through a department-wide working group organized by Deputy Secretary Blinken. Under Secretary Stengel and I cochair this group, which meets weekly to maintain a focus on Ukraine's successes in the face of overt Kremlin aggression and messaging distortion. Through this consultative process, we update our Embassies daily on current policy priorities, messages, and programs, and all State elements work to communicate our policy and support for Ukraine as one voice.

To reach the broader Russian-speaking population, the Department spokesperson's office last week launched a Russian-language version of its Twitter feed. Now, our official statements reach audiences in the region directly, without having to be interpreted by third parties. Along these lines, we are also engaging directly with independent media within Russia. State has placed interviews of more than a dozen Assistant Secretaries, Special Envoys, and other senior officials in such outlets this fiscal year.

Partnering with Others on Messaging

The U.S. is not alone in dealing with Russian disinformation. To correct untruths not only in Ukraine and Russia, but across Russian-speaking communities, we are joining forces with our partners in the EU to identify, analyze, and debunk Russian disinformation where and when we find it; highlight Ukraine's progress in building its democracy, fighting corruption, and advancing reform; bolster the Russian- speaking areas of Europe seeking to resist disinformation; and fortify transatlantic unity through institutions like NATO and the EU.

Through a group of messaging experts from like-minded countries – known as the "Friends of Ukraine" – we regularly consult on messaging campaigns, media trends, and Kremlin propaganda tactics. Friends of Ukraine (FoU) is a growing 20+ member network of governments and multilateral organizations committed to responding to disinformation in real time through multiple voices. Efforts by the FoU have helped to keep Ukraine on the front burner, even when the Kremlin's media machine has tried to distract its audiences with other topics.

NATO also is active in this area through its Strategic Communications Center of Excellence in Riga, Latvia. The newly-opened Center designs programs to advance StratCom doctrine development and standardization, conducts research and experimentation to find practical solutions to existing challenges, identifies lessons from StratCom operations, as well as enhances training and education efforts and interoperability throughout the Alliance.

And, our partners at The European External Action Service (EEAS), the EU's diplomatic corps, have started a new Strategic Communications unit, which directs public diplomacy messaging and programs throughout the Eastern Partnership countries. I visited Brussels recently and met with the leadership of this new unit, and was impressed by their team and the content and campaigns they are developing. We are committed to helping one another share content and distribute information through EU and U.S. channels, and this spring I hope to bring the State Department and EU teams together to enhance this much-needed collaboration.

Long Term: Building Capacity

While rapid response counter-messaging is a critical element of our strategy, local independent voices and a strong independent media are the real answer to free and democratic societies throughout the region. State Department and USAID programs support free media in the region to provide open, objective, accessible information to all. Exchange and assistance programs provide critical tools and increase access to a variety of local news sources, high-quality fact-based content, and honest investigative journalism.

We are proud of the exchange programs and "tech camps" we sponsor to link and train regional and transatlantic journalists and other opinion leaders. By November, we will have trained 120 "Tech Camp" alumni—60 in Prague and Riga and 60 more in Kyiv—who will go on to support strong independent journalism by sharing best practices and resources.

We are also working with the EU to cooperate on supporting the creation of new regional programs to support Russian-language media, based on the European Endowment for Democracy's (EED) Feasibility Study on Russian Language Media Initiatives.

Altogether, in FY15, the State Department and USAID allocated approximately $16 million to support independent media. Already, we have success stories that we are proud of including:

- Launching a yearlong investigative journalism training and exchange program for up to 75 journalists from the Baltics.

- The Regional Investigative Journalism Network, supported by USAID and DRL, which connects local investigative journalists throughout the region and helps them investigate and report on cases of corruption and misuse of government authority.

- And, the five-year Ukraine Media (U-Media) Project, which promotes the development of a free, vibrant and professional media sector in Ukraine and also serves as a watchdog in the public interest. The U-Media program has adapted to the changing context in Ukraine by promoting balanced political coverage across Ukraine through local content production, exchange visits, public discussions, and webcasts with special attention to the South and East. Local media partners also monitor and publicize intimidation and attacks on civic activists and journalists and government interference in independent media coverage of Ukrainian politics.

While training and exchanges are critical to our efforts, information is also impeded by the lack of communications infrastructure in many areas tied to Kremlin-sponsored programming.

To help build capacity, the Broadcasting Board of Governors' (BBG) new Russian-language news program, Current Time, is on air in nine countries via 25 major market commercial, satellite, and public media outlets.

Nearly two million viewers in Russia are watching Current Time online weekly, and BBG's digital media engagement has grown by an average of 2.5 million Russian-speakers per week.

A popular BBG program, "Footage v. Footage," is devoted to pointing out inconsistencies in Russian reporting and debunking myths.

BBG has also helped to bring about a contract with PBS Distribution for nearly 400 hours of Russian-language public media content to Ukraine, Lithuania and Estonia.

These stations will air these programs for Russian language speaking audiences starting in November of this year.

In late August, BBG also donated its recently developed "Fly Away FM System," which is suitable for use as low power FM transmitters.

While BBG's contributions, our exchanges, and public diplomacy programming are vital to our strategy against Kremlin disinformation, we must continue to ensure our commitments and support to our allies so that we continue to have a positive story to tell.

Resilience for the Future

Ultimately, countering disinformation is a security issue, especially when the goal of Russian disinformation and propaganda is to destabilize, distract, and divide our allies.

Addressing this problem is an important part of our diplomatic effort to promote a Europe whole, free, and at peace.

The Baltic States are primary targets of Russian disinformation, especially since all three – Latvia, Lithuania, and Estonia–are valued NATO Allies. Just as we are cooperating with them to counter Russian disinformation, we work together in the realm of collective defense.

The combination of our diplomatic efforts ensures that the U.S. not only has a positive story to tell, but that others will be able to hear it over the Kremlin's noise.

Despite Moscow's significant investment in disinformation, its efforts have limited effectiveness abroad. A Pew research poll published in August indicates that a median of only 30% of those polled outside of Russia see Russia favorably. Putin himself is viewed even less favorably, with only 24% of respondents having confidence that Putin will do the right thing in world affairs.

Here in the United States, we have not seen evidence that the Kremlin's misinformation has gained any traction: A recent Pew poll indicated 75% of Americans have no confidence in Putin to do the right thing in world affairs.

This reveals that even while Europe, and in particular Ukraine, works through tough challenges and fights disinformation, our work together continues to speak more loudly than Russia's meddling.

Mr. Chairman, Senator Shaheen, members of this committee, America's investment in public diplomacy is about more than fighting a single country.

It's about protecting the rules-based system across Europe and around the world. It's about saying no to borders changed by force, to big countries intimidating their neighbors or demanding a sphere of influence.

I thank this subcommittee for its bipartisan support and commitment to public diplomacy and to a Europe whole, free and at peace.

Countering Adversarial Propaganda Through Military Information Support Operations

Michael Lumpkin

Michael Lumpkin is the Assistant U.S. Secretary of Defense for Special Operations and Low-Intensity Conflict. He presented this policy review before the House Armed Services Committee on October 22, 2015.

Chairman Wilson, Ranking Member Langevin, and distinguished Members of the committee—I appreciate this opportunity today to discuss the Department of Defense's important supporting role to our government's efforts led by the Department of State in today's contested information environment. In advance I would like to thank you for this committee's support in this critical field. I will focus my remarks on the Department's supporting role in the U.S. Government effort and on the need to maintain agile authorities. I am very pleased to be joined today by the Brigadier General Moore, the Deputy Director for Global Operations in the Joint Staff operations directorate, to provide an operational perspective, and Major General Haas from U.S. Special Operations Command (USSOCOM), to discuss that command's role in ensuring the readiness of the Military Information Support Operations (MISO) force. I am here to discuss an aspect of our information operations capabilities that has received special attention from your committee and the other defense committees over the last few years: our military

information support operations force, which provides a critical influence capability

to meet the tactical and operational needs of military commands and provide

support to the overall strategic effort led by the State Department. As we begin

this hearing, I think it is important to note that I am not discussing the

Department's Public Affairs capabilities. Public affairs is a fully separate activity

from MISO and is directed at engaging the media and informing U.S. and other

Audiences.

As the principal civilian advisor to the Secretary of Defense on special operations

and low-intensity conflict matters, I directly support the Under Secretary of

Defense for Policy in her role as the Principal Staff Advisor for Information

Operations (IO). Additionally, in my role as the principal special operations

official within the senior management of the Department of Defense, I oversee

USSOCOM in its role as the joint proponent for military information support

operations. I am committed to ensuring that we develop, maintain, and employ the

proper IO capabilities to meet the tactical and operational requirements of military

commands and provide support to the strategic effort led by the Department of

State.

The Department's Supporting Role in the U.S. Government Effort.

Our MISO capabilities are unlike most capability sets in the Department of

Defense, and MISO requires additional oversight and coordination that is not

typically required of other Departmental activities. Whereas lethal and destructive

combat capabilities tend to belong exclusively to the Department, other U.S.

Government departments and agencies, such as the Broadcasting Board of

Governors and the Department of State, have capabilities, roles, and missions as

part of our Government's strategic communications efforts. This substantial

overlap in roles and capabilities leads leads to a need for close interagency

coordination and clear delineation of the appropriate roles for each organization.

This coordination is conducted within an overall U.S. Government

communications and engagement framework with global audiences. Within this

greater framework, the Department's MISO forces provide support to military

plans and operations, unique influence planning expertise, regional knowledge, and

the ability to advise, assist, and develop similar partner nation forces and

organizations.

The Department fully recognizes the overarching need for a strategic, whole-of-government effort in communications efforts. The Department of State generally leads U.S. Government communications and engagement efforts focused on foreign audiences. For example, the Department of State is home to the Center for Strategic Counterterrorism Communications (CSCC), which has the mission to "coordinate, orient, and inform government-wide strategic communications focused on violent extremists and terrorist organizations." The Department of Defense's efforts alone will not solve the challenge of this contested information environment and adversary propaganda. Instead the Department of Defense plays a critical role as a contributor and partner to the whole-of-government effort led by the State Department.

The Department also recognizes the military necessity of operating in the information environment. Our combatant commanders have clear military objectives to maintain the stability and security of their regions, in concert with other U.S. Government efforts, and this involves operating in the information environment. Additionally, the Department can offer unique military capabilities that can play a critical role in achieving overall communications objectives. These types of actions are not done, or conceived, in competition with other U.S. departments and agencies but in coordination with them.

As we employ our MISO forces in environments outside areas of military hostilities, we will always maintain military command and control of our forces and operate in a manner that achieves mutual support between U.S. departments and agencies. At the national level, we will partner with the lead agency, usually the Department of State, and provide unique Defense capabilities to support the coordination and synchronization of a whole-of-government effort that combines public diplomacy, public affairs, U.S. international media, information operations, and other capabilities. At the request of the State Department, the Department has provided five military IO and MISO planners to the cell within CSCC that coordinates our national efforts against the Islamic State of Iraq and the Levant (ISIL), and we currently maintain an additional MISO planner within the State Department to support planning in other geographic areas.

Overseas, we fully acknowledge the role of Chiefs of Mission and ensure that our military operations are fully coordinated. We always ensure we provide a complementary capability, and a capability that is not duplicative with those of other departments and agencies..

The Department also builds partnerships with other U.S. Government

organizations. A key initiative that has emerged over the last year has been the

Department's partnership with various entities of the Broadcasting Board of

Governors (BBG). Spearheaded by a pilot project at U.S. Pacific Command, our

relationship with BBG exemplifies the necessary whole-of-government approach

to key challenges such as countering violent extremist ideology and exposing

hostile propaganda.

Tailoring an appropriate menu of Policy Authorities

There are nuanced distinctions between informing, educating, persuading, and

influencing audiences using information. The Department's efforts span all of

these activities depending on the specific military mission. The key question

relates to the boundaries and limitations on each department or agency's role in

this space. The Department needs flexibility to be able to keep up with the nature

of today's transnational threats and evolving technology. This flexibility, however,

will not diminish the Department's oversight of MISO. We will make certain that

our operations are tied to clear military objectives contained in theater campaign or

other operational plans, that all actions are fully consistent with applicable law, including the covert action statute, and that we have achieved the necessary

coordination with interagency partners.

The requirements for MISO capabilities are increasingly pressing, as our

adversaries and competitors, both State and non-State actors, rely heavily on

propaganda to achieve their aims. This is most evident with the sophisticated and

well-resourced propaganda campaigns being waged by ISIL and by the Russian

Federation becoming more and more aggressive in Eastern Europe. ISIL uses

information on a global scale to recruit, facilitate foreign fighter flow, finance, and

gain tacit support for their violent agenda. Similarly, Russian propaganda seeks to

intimidate or undermine our allies and partners outside of areas of hostilities.

Many of these activities are happening online and over social media.

These trends highlight a critical role for MISO in places outside areas of hostilities,

with clear military missions supporting broader, non-military U.S. Government

efforts. The Department cannot address these challenges effectively by itself;

instead, in a supporting role, we will partner with our interagency colleagues and

provide our unique MISO capabilities as part of a whole-of-government solution.

Additionally, the Department's MISO capabilities and authorities must remain agile enough to reach our target audiences through whatever their preferred form

of communication; whether it is radio, television, internet, or whatever

technologies emerge in the future.

As you are aware, our Military Information Support Operations programs have

been an item of special congressional interest since 2010. In the past, the MISO

communities saw their budgets and authorities grow in support of Operations

IRAQI and ENDURING FREEDOM. These growing budgets and their associated

activities resulted in increasing concerns over their scope, effectiveness, command

and control, and integration with other U.S. efforts. The Department has a clear

role for MISO to change the behavior of appropriate foreign target audiences

through dissemination of information tailored to influence in support of military

objectives. We have endeavored to ensure we stay within this role, and we

appreciate the Committee's support.

Over the past five years, the Department has worked closely with the Congress to

improve and institutionalize appropriate oversight of this mission area. We have

endeavored to address congressional concerns fully in this area while improving

our capabilities to meet current challenges. My Information Operations

Directorate, which enables our effective oversight, is one of the largest directorates in my organization. Over the last five years, we have emplaced improved fiscal controls and scoped our budget requests to ensure a clear and direct linkage from strategy to task to resource. We have made positive strides in the area of oversight, and we appreciate the increasingly positive language and support over the last year from this Committee and others that reflects increased confidence in our oversight. We also understand the concerns that have arisen in the past regarding the scope and effectiveness of some programs that we have since terminated. We appreciate the Committee's support in this effort. I would ask your continued support for the Department's role in this critical space, especially as we craft new programs that are threat-based, scoped to critical audiences, and developed with clear measures of effectiveness that reflect their support of military objectives and the overall State Department's-led strategic effort.

Building the future force

The imperative to stay abreast of increasing technological change and our adversaries' rapid adaptation of technology demands that the Department use a thoughtful, strategic approach to achieve success against a mix of adversaries. Simply trying to match our adversaries "tweet" for "tweet" or matching website for website would be both fiscally irresponsible and operationally ineffective. Instead, the Department must rely on the skills of its human capital to develop thoughtful, well-constructed plans and partnerships with other U.S. Government departments and agencies and with foreign partners, and to leverage a variety of means to disrupt the adversary's narrative, expose its contradictions and falsehoods, and ultimately bring credible, persuasive, and truthful information to audiences who often have significantly differing perceptions and cultural norms than our own. The Department is currently evaluating whether we are appropriately leveraging a range of emerging technologies to the maximum extent possible to gain an advantage over our adversaries.

As the Office of the Secretary of Defense exercises our oversight role, we will develop the future MISO force using the following general guidance:

First and foremost, we will continue to ensure the proper military command and control and effective organizations for our operations. Having clear military command and control linkages helps ensure synchronization and mutual support between the range of activities by each combatant command and its subordinate components. The continual evolution of communications technology will likely require additional organizational innovation as we seek to maintain our capability to influence in an "always-on," dynamic, and interactive social media environment. Second, we will ensure that the Department's operations in this arena are focused on designated threat groups and adversaries or support military-to-military engagement. Information activities broadly directed at large global or regional audiences are more appropriately conducted by Public Diplomacy, Public Affairs, and the BBG's media activities.

Third, we will seek the right balance between military, government civilian, and contracted capabilities. We know most of our information activities will require long-term effort. As technology and the way society utilizes the emerging communications means continue to evolve, we foresee the continual need to bring new skill sets into our MISO force.

Fourth, we will continue to maintain and build upon the partnerships we have created with our interagency partners. We will sustain the high level of trust and cooperation we already have built in support of Department of State-led efforts.

Fifth, we will seek to apply greater interagency support to our operations to ensure our operations are focused and to provide better assessment of their effectiveness.

Finally, we will continue to demonstrate the strength of our oversight and the transparency in our reporting to the congressional defense committees. We will develop and apply the right metrics and continue to bring our candid assessment back to you as to what has worked and what lessons we have learned.

Ultimately, the concepts we bring forward to you will be clearly linked with intelligence analysis and demonstrate how we will respond and defeat threats in the information environment, using greater precision and rigor in our planning. In this sense, our future planning should be similar in scope and detail to what our other special operations forces do in their counterterrorism missions.

Conclusion

In response to congressional concerns over the last six years, we have emplaced the right team and processes to provide oversight of the Department's MISO force. We recognize that even in support to military operations in areas of hostilities, the

Department's capabilities and activities must be coordinated with a strategic U.S. Government effort that is led by the Department of State. Within this role, the Department will seek to maintain agile authorities as technologies evolve and our adversaries adapt. Furthermore, we will continue to develop our forces to be proficient in the current and projected communication environment.

Thank you for your support, and I pledge to ensure our MISO capabilities will be ready to play their vital role in support of commanders and their operations and as an integral part of our Nation's comprehensive efforts to counter adversary propaganda.

The MISO Force:

Organizing, Training and Equipping U.S. Special Operations Forces for Information Operations

Christopher Haas

Major General Christopher Haas is Director of Force Management and Development, U.S. Special Operations Command. He presented this overview of U.S. Special Forces Command's Military Information Support Operations infrastructure before the House Armed Services Committee on October 22, 2015.

INTRODUCTION

Mr. Chairman, and distinguished Members of the committee, thank you for the opportunity to come before you today to discuss US Special Operations Command's (USSOCOM) manning, training, and equipping of the Military Information Support Operations (MISO) force. While I will cover the broader aspects of each of those responsibilities, I will comment from a perspective of countering our adversaries' influence efforts. Preparing our MISO forces for current and future conflict is a critical role for USSOCOM. The USSOCOM Commander places a great deal of emphasis on operating in the human domain, which is particularly important in our current conflicts and is the focus of our MISO forces. As Assistant Secretary of Defense Lumpkin previously mentioned, the extensive propaganda efforts employed by both the Islamic State of Iraq and the Levant (ISIL) and the Russian Federation make USSOCOM's role in manning, training and equipping the MISO force even more critical. We have made significant improvements in all three areas over the last decade, but there is considerable work remaining— particularly in improving our MISO force's capability through training to counter our adversaries' influence on the world-wide web which they currently extensively exploit.

MANNING THE MISO FORCE TO OPTIMIZE ITS IMPACT

The first of USSOCOM's roles is to adequately man the MISO force. Without the right number of skilled people in the right positions, the MISO force cannot accomplish its mission. Overall end strength of the two active duty groups is 1051 officers and enlisted MISO Soldiers. The active MISO officer corps is 224 assigned against 204 billets and is appropriately manned at the Captain, Lieutenant Colonel and Colonel levels. The aggregate strength of the active duty officer force is 112 percent, which is comparable to other branches. This end strength will be adjusted by management tools such as selected early retirement, and promotion reductions. The majorities of officers are serving at the operational level (55%) and at Special Operations Forces commands (16%). Our noncommissioned officers are also appropriately manned at the Staff Sergeant or E-6 levels and above; however, the inventory of Sergeants (E-5) is below authorized levels. The strength of our active duty groups' enlisted force is 872 assigned against 1295 billets, a shortage of 423 Soldiers.

The total active duty officer and enlisted strength is 70 percent, with more than 88 percent serving at the operational level. While this is not an ideal situation at the enlisted level, our projections indicate the training pipeline should have active duty MISO groups fully manned by FY 2019. Also, our FY2015 retention statistics indicate that retention efforts for the two active duty groups are retaining enough quality personnel to avoid any degradation to their current capabilities. The United States Army John F. Kennedy Special Warfare Center and School is exploring additional opportunities through the Army Special Operations Forces Recruiting Battalion to recruit more Officer and NCO candidates. These opportunities include possible retention incentives targeting enlisted Soldiers in the ranks of sergeant to sergeant first class with qualifying language scores. Additionally, the active duty groups are participating in recruiting events with the Army Special Operations Recruiting Battalion that are specifically targeted to increase the number of officer and enlisted candidates for MISO selection and assessment.

An additional aspect of manning the force is placing personnel in an optimum force structure. In 2014, the United States Army Special Operations Command re-organized the United States Special Forces Command from exclusively manning, training and equipping Special Forces units to now include Civil Affairs and the two active duty MISO Groups. This streamlining of effort, now represents the largest, newest and most adaptive Army Division providing the Geographic Combatant Commanders and Theater Special Operations Commanders the forces necessary to accomplish their assigned missions. This command relationship has already provided synergy to operations in AFRICOM, CENTCOM and EUCOM areas of responsibility, such as with operations against Joseph Kony and the Lord's Resistance Army in Central Africa where MISO, Special Forces and Civil Affairs elements have enabled partner nation efforts resulting in dramatic gains in combating this adversary.

TRAINING THE MISO FORCE – ADAPTING TO THE MISSION

The complexity of mission and the expertise required to carry out MISO missions has shaped and extended the training program for MISO soldiers. Prior to any formal training, service members seeking to enter the MISO force undergo an extensive selection process— a process designed to identify those able to function under physical and mental stress. Assessment and selection is a ten-day process with eight selection cycles per year. All candidates are assessed against the core SOF attributes—integrity, courage, perseverance, personal responsibility, professionalism, adaptability, teamwork, and capability, as well as validated physical and mental occupational performance standards. All events are designed to measure specific attributes required to posture a candidate for success in the MISO field. Candidates are isolated and undergo both physical and mental stressors to measure problem solving abilities, resilience and stamina.

Following selection into the MISO career field, our Soldiers attend a 5-phase, 42-week training program. This training includes extensive studies in MISO planning, linguistics, and cultural knowledge, interagency support, media development and dissemination, effective analysis and assessments and translator/interpreter management. The end state of the training

pipeline is to produce a skilled MISO soldier capable of planning, executing and measuring

MISO across the full spectrum of operations in all environments in support of joint, interagency,

multinational or coalition operations. These soldiers are capable of operating in both

technologically superior and austere environments. They are responsive and adaptive to

asymmetrical challenges; adaptive and comfortable with ambiguity. They are culturally aware,

regionally focused and language-capable. Two areas of this MISO training that differentiate

them from other US Government capabilities are the focus on language and culture as well as a

focus on influence principles. I'd like to highlight these two unique characteristics. The language

and cultural priorities are based upon MISO force demand and are oriented on critical regions of

the world. While it can be challenging to produce fluent language speakers in many of the more

challenging languages, the benefits of understanding language and culture are critical in

determining how a culture communicates or the value a culture places on relationships. These

shared assumptions drive meaning within any group. Linguistic and cultural knowledge provide

an insight which is critical to conducting effective influence operations. The extensive training

that our Soldiers receive enables them to leverage the cultural nuances of influence. They learn

when it is most appropriate to use an emotional appeal or a rational argument, what the best mix

of media is to convey a certain type of argument, and what symbols are relevant in conveying the

specific message. This training, combined with linguistic and cultural understanding, makes

MISO a true SOF capability and a distinct asset within the Department of Defense. In regards to

training volume, in FY14 and FY15, our training base has maintained an 80 percent graduation

rate.

As you well know, our adversaries use the Internet to contact and recruit followers, gain financial support and to spread propaganda and misinformation. As I mentioned in my introduction, we continue to adapt to emerging requirements. The current conflicts have identified that we have a need to continue expanding our MISO training, primarily with regards to the Web. Through the Joint requirements process, USCentral, USPacific, USAfrican, and USEuropean Commands all identified gaps in regard to MISO use of the Web. SOCOM is in the process of developing a comprehensive plan capturing all aspects of this requirement; a key aspect of the requirement being training. This training will incorporate social media use, online advertising, web metrics, and web design, among many other topics. Such a training solution will also enable us to stop being so dependent upon a contracted solution. In the interest of managing expectations however, such training cannot happen overnight and we may always need some level of contracted support in translation and IT expertise. We will be dependent upon contractors in the short term as we train the force. While this occurs we will seek to accomplish significant on the job training and learning from the contracted expertise to augment our training efforts. Ultimately, we will find the right balance between what tasks the MISO force can execute and those requiring contracted expertise to accomplish.

EQUIPPING THE MISO FORCE – STAYING CURRENT

Maintaining a current MISO equipment capability to meet operational requirements is an ongoing effort, but one USSOCOM is well positioned to meet. We have been upgrading our MISO production and dissemination capability continuously to meet the force's requirements. We have a state-of-the-art Media Production Center at Fort Bragg, with the capability to provide for print, audio, and video product development. The Center also includes redundant archival features to preserve all past and current MISO planning and production efforts. Some of the current deployable equipment includes: the flyaway broadcast system, a radio, TV, and cellular broadcast capability, next generation loudspeaker systems, and an interoperable responsive short or long term mass printing capability. These systems are fielded and in operation by our MISO forces supporting commands around the world.

We are also constantly exploring and developing future MISO capabilities to ensure we meet the emerging needs of the Geographic Combatant Commands and Theater Special Operations Commands. This process involves researching emerging technologies, assessing the needs of the MISO force, and MISO systems development, with integrated testing and evaluation. All equipment decisions are made in accordance with the USSOCOM Commander's prioritized resourcing guidance, developed from an objective mission and gap analysis of USSOCOM mission sets. Some of the future capabilities we are in the process of developing are the distributable audio media system, a leaflet-like system with embedded pre-recorded audio and/or audio-visual messages, an upgraded version of the flyaway broadcast system mentioned earlier with a 97% size/weight reduction, and the long range broadcast system; a pod-mounted radio, TV, and cellular broadcast system on manned and unmanned aircraft allowing MISO message broadcast out to 100 miles. We are also in the process of testing an Internet Production Capability (IPC), which will be a fully integrated suite of work stations designed to perform web research, data capture, message product development, and web-based message delivery. The IPC will provide a secure means of navigating the Web, a means to conduct social media analysis, provide multiple methods to deliver online messages, and provide the ability to monitor real-time measures of effectiveness and adjust MISO programs/campaigns shortly after launching on social media.

USSOCOM welcomes the committee's support regarding technology demonstrations to assess innovative, new technologies for MISO. This is timely in light of the previously mentioned comprehensive plan USSOCOM is developing to address the Geographic Combatant Command gaps regarding MISO use of the Web. This plan will include a detailed analysis of the equipment component as part of the solution. Such analysis will address what equipment is needed in various locations to support operations. Congressional support will greatly assist in jump-starting that aspect of the plan and will ensure our force remains current and is able to accomplish assigned missions in support of our National Security objectives. While we will develop detailed plans, the web-based technologies we are exploring are less reliant on home station basing and more flexible in nature to provide support on-site to the Geographic Combatant Commands and Theater Special Operations Commands and reflect our commitment to providing MISO support to the Geographic Combatant Commands.

CONCLUSIONS

In conclusion, once again I would like to thank the committee members for the opportunity to provide information in regard to USSOCOM's role in manning, training and equipping its MISO force. USSOCOM stands ready to counter our adversaries in any environment, including the information environment. All shortfalls are being addressed and mitigated through the creative and adaptive use of current personnel and equipment, leveraging contracted services and personnel where appropriate. Our MISO forces monitor, assess and evaluate media trends in the information environment. We recognize the importance of operating in this space and believe we clearly have a role of engaging on the worldwide web focused specifically on the threat in support of military objectives as part of the whole-of-government approach. The mission is challenging – the information environment moves faster than ever before and supporting technology evolves at an even faster pace. Our adversaries are currently using propaganda and misinformation to great effect, often with a mix of sophisticated technology and overt brutality. This trend will not be deterred, and will only accelerate if not contested. It is a safe assumption that future adversaries will observe, learn, and adapt new strategies. We must move forward with clarity of purpose and focus our uniquely qualified non-kinetic resources to combat our nation's enemies.

I also thank you for your continued support of our SOF personnel and their families; the tremendous demands we have placed upon them requires a continued commitment to provide for their well-being and support their mission success.

German Navy SEALs
Kampfschwimmer Naval Commandos

By Ingo Mathe

German naval commandos are called Kampfschwimmer or "combat swimmers". These German navy counterparts to the US Navy SEALs are Germany's oldest Special Operations Forces. The Kampfschwimmer roots go back to World War II.

Today's Kampfschwimmer formations are heavily involved in international operations against terrorism, including missions in the mountains of Afghanistan. This e-book is written by a German Navy lieutenant who serves as a Kampfschwimmer team leader -- the equivalent of a US Navy SEAL platoon leader.

"German Navy SEALs" is a profile of the Kampfschwimmer units. The e-book covers the history of the Kampfschwimmer beginning with the World War II era; describes their organization, command structure, capabilities and training; discusses their cooperation with US Navy SEALS and other Special Operations Forces; and their role in German and NATO operational planning.

Other German Special Operations Forces are also briefly discussed.

German Navy "SEALs": *Kampfschwimmer* Naval Commandos is available exclusively as an e-book for Kindle.

5,400 words

To order please visit www.teamultimedia.com

Countering Adversary Propaganda Through Special Information Operations

Charles Moore

Brigadier General Charles Moore is Deputy Director for Global Operations, U.S. Joint Staff.
On October 22, 2015 Brigadier General Moore presented the House Armed Services Committee with this briefing on U.S. Military information operations designated to counter adversary propaganda.

Mr. Chairman, Ranking member, and distinguished members of the committee, thank you for the opportunity to appear before you today to discuss the actions we in the Department of Defense are taking to counter the propaganda campaigns of our adversaries.

In order to effectively achieve our military objectives and end states, Information Operations MUST be inherently integrated with all military plans and activities in order to influence and ultimately alter the behavior of our adversaries and their supporters. Simultaneously, we must defend ourselves and friends from the influence operations undertaken by our enemies. Recent events in the CENTCOM and EUCOM regions demonstrate how ISIL and Russia are using IO campaigns to influence, shape, and define the conflict. Both of these actors possess the resources and organizational structure to operate effectively in the information environment. In regards to ISIL, we assess that this organization utilizes the information domain to recruit, fund, spread their ideology and control their operations. With respect to Russia, we have seen the employment of "hybrid warfare" (which includes regular, irregular, and aggressive information operations actions) to illegally seize Crimea, foment separatist fever in several sovereign nations, and conduct operations in Syria.

There are several capabilities available to Combatant Commanders that help to achieve our objectives while minimizing the effects of enemy Information Operations and propaganda. But, the most common is the employment of our Military Information Support Operations forces or MISO forces. MISO personnel have the training and cultural understanding required to assess hostile propaganda activities and propose unique solutions that directly support our ability to achieve our military objectives.

MISO forces, operating from a U.S. Embassy, an operational task force, or a component headquarters are employed to execute DoD missions that support: named operations, geographic combatant commander (GCC) Theater Security Cooperation efforts, and public diplomacy. How Combatant Commanders employ their military information operations capabilities, to counter adversarial propaganda, is what I understand you want to focus our discussions on today.

MISO forces are currently deployed to locations around the globe, working closely with other U.S. Government departments, agencies and partner nations to address threats specific to their regions. For example, MISO forces are currently deployed to 21 U.S. embassies, working with country teams and interagency partners to challenge adversary IO actions and support broader U.S. government actions and goals. MISO forces, along with other advise and assist efforts, conduct training with some of our closest partners in order to make them more capable of conducting their own operations. Finally, our MISO forces use a variety of mediums (for example: cyber, print, TV, and radio) to disseminate information in a manner that will change perceptions and subsequently the behavior of the target audiences.

Unfortunately, as this is an unclassified hearing, the specific examples I can discuss are limited. But, I do want to provide some brief examples of the efforts our MISO forces are currently undertaking around the world.

In Central Command, MISO efforts are focused on challenging the actions of Violent Extremist organizations. For example, in Iraq, MISO forces are conducting an advise and assist role to help Iraqi forces learn how to develop indigenous Military Information Support

Operations and counter-propaganda activities. Central Command's online influence strategy is used to counter adversary narratives, shape conditions in their AOR, and to message specific target audiences. These operations include using existing web and social media platforms to support military objectives by shaping perceptions. For example, Central Command is active on Facebook, Twitter, YouTube and other online communications platforms for its Middle Eastern and Central Asian audiences; using these forums to highlight ISIL atrocities, coalition responses to ISIL activities and to highlight Coalition successes. They remain vigilant and stand ready to adapt and reshape their approach as new dissemination platforms potentially emerge.

European Command's efforts include exposing Russian mistruths and their concerted efforts to mislead European audiences as to their true intentions. We are in the final stages of staffing the European Reassurance MISO Program (ERMP), which will provide expanded authorities to conduct MISO training and in some cases, messaging support, to our partners in the region. Additionally, EUCOM is preparing to launch a pilot program in 2016 that will leverage social media to deliver information to critical target audiences. EUCOM is also looking to expand its partnership with the Broadcasting Board of Governors to further improve its information dissemination capabilities.

Pacific Command has already expanded their partnership with the Broadcasting Board of Governors to develop a new initiative that expands existing BBG counterterrorism efforts. This initiative, named BenarNews.org, was designed to address the gap left by the termination of PACOM's counterterrorism websites. Pacific Command is synchronizing a holistic counterterrorism effort consisting of BenarNews, interactive internet activities which target specific enemy actors, on line military magazines, and Military Information Support Teams.

The bottom line is that regardless of the region of the world or the enemies that we face, the DoD understands the criticality of countering an adversary's and their supporters' confidence, conviction, will and decision making while shaping behaviors supportive of our military objectives. We understand that these actions must be taken while not exceeding the authorities we have been granted and while always operating within the boundaries the Department has been given and with close coordination among our interagency partners.

Finally, I also want to express my appreciation for the support this committee has given acknowledging DoD's need to operate "across all available media to most effectively reach target audiences" and for your unwavering support of our men and women in uniform.

Thank you again for the opportunity to appear this afternoon, I look forward to answering your questions.

German Navy F124 Frigates
Unique and Indispensable Air Defense Capabilities

By Andreas Uhl

The German navy's F124 air-defense frigates (also known as the Sachsen Class frigates) compare very favorably with the U.S. Navy Aegis cruisers and destroyers. No other warship of the western world can boast – as the F124 frigate does – three different guided missile systems which optimally translate the concept of defense-in-depth / layered defense into action.

This article describes and analyzes the air and missile defense capabilities of the F124 Class, including details of its sensor technology; and describes its role in NATO and Coalition naval operations.

The author, Andreas Uhl, is a German naval officer with extensive experience in the maritime air and missile defense sector.

F124 Frigates is published in cooperation with Marine Forum magazine, and is available exclusively as an e-book. Please click the link on this page to purchase and download from Amazon.com.

To order please visit www.teamultimedia.com

Shaping Global Opinion: The Role of the Broadcasting Board of Governors

Matthew Armstrong

Matthew Armstrong is a member of the Broadcasting Board of Governors. He briefed the House Armed Services Committee on the role of this organization on October 22, 2015

Mr. Chairman and Members of the Subcommittee, thank you for inviting me to speak to the unique role the Broadcasting Board of Governors (BBG) and United States international media play in advancing our national interests.

I am pleased to join today's panel alongside my colleagues from the Department of Defense (DoD). It is appropriate, and important, that we remain vigilant to the ways in which information and ideas impact our national security. Every day, around the world, we face adversaries and challengers whose primary weapon is not kinetic, but the expert deployment, and at times active suppression, of information.

In today's increasingly interconnected world, responding to the global explosion of information must be a key focus of U.S. foreign policy. Each day, the voices and messages of our friends and foes alike travel and impact beyond familiar political borders with the press of a "share" button. Communities and conversations in the digital space are created without limit to a specific geographical area. As technology continues to develop, cross-border communications and dissemination of information will only increase.

While the information revolution offers the world a plethora of opportunity, particularly those who have lacked a voice either locally and on the global stage, it also provides challenges. In just the past five years, we have seen vivid examples where both state and non-state actors have effectively used information to challenge the United States, our values of democracy and freedom, and the very existence of objective truth.

From Crimea, to Syria, Northern Nigeria, and Southeast Asia, propaganda and censorship have resurged in our increasingly networked world to foment hate and confusion, monitor and suppress dissent, activate acts of terror and roll-back hard- won freedoms. Actors from ISIL to Russia to China are using information not just to "win the news cycle," but to shape the very choices of statecraft.

U.S. foreign policy cannot be effective if we do not appreciate how information shapes the actions of policymakers, institutions, and everyday citizens on the street. The simple truth is that today's media has the power to reach through the screen to activate audiences to action – or to suppress them. Failing to recognize this fact limits the effectiveness of our foreign policy.

U.S. international media advances U.S. national interests by engaging audiences that are critical to advancing democratic values through open and free exchanges of information.

The BBG oversees all nonmilitary international media supported by the U.S. government, including the Voice of America (VOA), the Office of Cuba Broadcasting (OCB), and BBG-funded grantees Radio Free Europe/Radio Liberty, Inc. (RFE/RL), Radio Free Asia (RFA) and the Middle East Broadcasting Networks, Inc. (MBN). We inform, engage, and connect people around the world in support of freedom and democracy.

Throughout U.S. international media's long history, the tools and goals have been consistent: delivering consistently accurate, reliable and credible reporting that opens minds and stimulates debate in closed societies and those where free media are not yet fully established – especially where local media fails to inform and empower its citizens.

The mission of the Broadcasting Board of Governors is unique. We are a 24/7 global media organization, built for a global mission. BBG radio, television, Internet, and mobile programs reach more than 215 million people each week, in sixty-one languages.

As a journalism organization, our mission is to empower people with both the truth and the context of local, regional, and global affairs, as well as through news from the United States. Our journalists don't just present the news, they unpack the news to provide their audiences with a greater understanding of their world and what is happening. Great journalism – the stories that stick with an audience – shows, often indirectly and subtly, how democracies should work. Great journalism helps audiences understand how democratic accountability, rule of law (not rule by law), human rights, and human security should work, and the differences between the vision of democratic ideals and the reality, so that audiences understand the contrast.

The unique difference of the BBG is not only that we do the news in sixty-one different languages, but also that we prioritize our content to impact our strategic audiences. Many of our reporters are not only from our target markets, but they also maintain extensive networks in them and speak as locals. They don't parachute in. We know the audiences, what they need to know, and how the story is best told. This is what makes the BBG networks, including VOA, unique. We are called upon, as enshrined in our founding legislation, to operate in markets until "private information dissemination is found to be adequate." Virtually by definition, we target markets that are hard to reach and, at best, under served by accessible reliable independent media. There is no other agency or corporation like us – that puts the audience first, and that actively builds true, independent media markets, in order to one day not be needed. We use future redundancy as a primary measure of success.

President Obama said in his recent speech at the U.N. General Assembly: "The strength of nations depends on the success of their people – their knowledge, their innovation, their imagination, their creativity, their drive, their opportunity – and that, in turn, depends upon individual rights and good governance and personal security."

By unleashing the power of professional journalism, we open up new markets for independent media and, in doing so, challenge the governments, institutions, and non-state actors who would manipulate facts to limit choice or infringe the rights of their people. Accurate news not only informs the public, it allows individuals to aspire to freedom by offering them a platform from which to make decisions based on what is verifiably true – rather than on what their governments may tell them. In short, by exporting the power of a free press we fuel and sustain the exchange of ideas and the struggle for individual thought and freedom – the very building blocks of democratic freedom.

The VOA Charter, which is enshrined in our enabling legislation, mandates that our programs "present the policies of the United States clearly and effectively, and… also present responsible discussions and opinion on these policies." In this way we are a part of broader U.S. public diplomacy, a means by which the U.S. Government can articulate and explain its policies and actions, and through which Congress and other constituencies can present alternate views.

Our journalism exposes corruption and abuse, and empowers our audience to root it out. When we cover the success of free and open elections, as we have recently in Nigeria, we educate audiences on how opposition parties can seek power peacefully through the ballot. When we help repressed voices talk about their future, as we do in Iran, we show how communities can solve problems on their own.

And when we train the lens on our own challenges, for example by covering the protests surrounding Ferguson, Missouri and the subsequent national debate on racial equality, the Detroit bankruptcy, or differing views on key foreign policy initiatives, such as the recent negotiations with Iran, we allow the world to see democracy not as an abstraction, but as a constantly evolving work in progress. This reporting shows the strength of our democracy – the identification of problems, the ability to air our differences in peaceful, respectful ways in line with the rule of law – and gives the opportunity to dive into often unfamiliar concepts to our audiences, such as accountability of civil authorities, what a grand jury is, and how a legal system can work. Even talking about how – and why – Americans go about paying parking tickets can open the eyes of our audiences.

Journalism is a powerful force for change. By acting as the "foreign domestic media" we play a critical role in the lives of audiences, as a news source that provides them with information, in their local language and relevant to their daily lives, that helps them make critical decisions. Decisions on their tolerance for local corruption. Decisions on whether to believe disinformation or form an opinion on fact-based information. Decisions on whether to be connected to the world or remain isolated from it.

U.S. International Media and U.S. Foreign Policy

Today, with so much of the world awash in information, the BBG's role is changing. As our adversaries have embraced the opportunities to engage and influence audiences using new tools and techniques, the BBG has made changes as well.

Our success no longer depends on our unique global reach, but also on the intensity of the BBG's relationships with its audiences, the extent to which they share and comment on our news and information and, ultimately, how they influence local knowledge and thought.

The impact of U.S. international media for the next decade is based on our ability to be an influential news and information source in this dynamic 21st century information environment. Under the leadership of our new CEO, the BBG is aggressively moving along five core themes to be the 21st century media organization the tax payers – and the Government – demands.

First, the BBG is accelerating our shift toward engaging audiences on digital platforms, especially utilizing the power of video, mobile, and social networks. We must be on the platform, in the format, and providing the content the audience needs – be it radio, television, or mobile tools and social media. To be clear, this is not just one-way dissemination, but also the empowering and encouraging of their participation in the conversations.

Second, we are rapidly expanding coordination and content-sharing across the BBG's five interdependent networks in order to cover and report on the stories that matter to audiences and markets that increasingly transcend political borders and languages. For instance, this will allow us to more effectively share our coverage of the Middle East with interested audiences in Indonesia and Russia, or issues surrounding Chinese investment in Africa with audiences across Latin America.

Third, the BBG is concentrating its efforts in five key issue areas where we can be most effective in support of our mission. These five areas are Russia; covering violent extremism; the widening regional influence of Iran; China, not only in the South China Sea region, but also in Africa and Latin America; and, the continuing struggle for democratic rights in Cuba.

Fourth, we are evolving to an organization actively engaged in curating, commissioning, and acquiring content. This is about more than just internal capacity. There are new generations of compelling storytellers, such as the youth in many of our markets, documentarians and journalists that engage their peers every day on digital platforms.

Finally, in the past, the BBG was asked to maximize our potential reach, as befitting a broadcasting organization with a broadcasting mentality. We "paid back" the American people whenever we powered up a new transmitter or launched a new program over satellite. Today, we are focusing on impact over reach; specifically by putting the audience first in how we collect, create and distribute news and information.

Now, let me touch upon three key challenges that may be of interest to the Committee.

Responding to Russia

The Kremlin has demonstrated the use of propaganda and disinformation as a tool of foreign policy, as well as maintaining support at home. By doing so, the Kremlin has built a house of cards that is susceptible to the truth and transparency. We see the constant statements and laws to shut down the freedom of speech and the freedom to listen in Russia. We see the same in the Kremlin's second greatest export – propaganda and obfuscation – that encourages audiences to "Question More" - to the point of not trusting anyone or thinking independently.

Countering Russian propaganda is not a proactive strategy; it is a reactionary posture predisposed to responding to the Kremlin's initiative. It allows the Kremlin the space to be proactive in disseminating disinformation to distract and obfuscate reality to manufacture blame and mask their own activities.

The BBG engages key audiences in Russia, the Russian periphery, and globally to provide them with the realities about Russian, and US activities, and, importantly, their context. Like elsewhere, we want our audiences to be empowered by facts and to think, to see the 'say-do' gaps of their leaders, which we have found over the decades to be a successful strategy for countering propaganda. For instance, RFE/RL continues to ramp up DIGIM, its new social-media driven digital reporting and engagement service, which includes the "Footage vs. Footage" feature, a daily video product that compares and contrasts how Russian media and global media report on the same events, providing the facts of a case and pointing out inconsistencies in Russian reporting.

We engage the audience's – often silently held – interests and concerns. The fundamental question that Former Soviet Union (FSU) citizens are considering is "Are we headed in the right direction?" They are weighing whether Putin's political and social reality is where they want to raise their children, start or grow a business, get an education; these are pocketbook and core questions that speak to hopes and dreams. In other words, the future media environment is not just about countering Kremlin propaganda, but a campaign for the future of the region.

Covering Violent Extremism

Extremist narratives too often go unaddressed within local media environments and digital echo chambers. These narratives are often tied to extremists' alleged religious virtue and organizational invincibility, with a toxic additive of anti- American conspiracy theories.

Our journalism exposes the gap between rhetoric and reality – ideologically and organizationally – of extremist groups. We do this through objective reporting that adheres to the highest standards of professional journalism. By covering violent extremism, we expose it for what it is.

Extremist groups have excelled at re-centering the news cycle on their violence. The BBG offers audiences more than coverage of violence through programming on positive alternative visions for the world to build support for more stable local and regional communities.

While other parts of the government directly support civil society, the BBG is uniquely positioned to elevate moderate voices – from the street to the elites. To cover local issues of concern, and provide constructive outlets for communities to discuss the issues that matter to them. For example, MBN's 30-minute, weekly documentary series "Delusional Paradise" presents firsthand accounts, obtained through original interviews, of families and communities that have suffered at the hands of ISIL. The program includes compelling accounts of families, in their own words, who have lost loved ones both due to ISIL recruitment and attacks, including the first interview with the Jordanian pilot's family.

Internet Freedom

A third prominent challenge for us is the fundamental importance of information freedom.

This is an enduring and central role for the BBG. Almost 75 years ago, President Roosevelt gave his 'Four Freedoms' speech that symbolized America's war aims and gave hope to a war-wearied people because they knew they were fighting for
freedom. His first freedom was of speech and expression everywhere in the world.

Today information freedom means the freedom for people around the world to be informed, to engage and connect with one another and ultimately use that information to change their lives and the lives of their community for the better.

I have followed, worked on, and blogged about public diplomacy and strategic communication issues for more than a decade. And I've been privileged enough to combine these experiences in my work on the Broadcasting Board of Governors.

I recall the rush when early bloggers in formerly closed societies pushed the envelope, and blogged about things their governments would rather see kept quiet.

At the time, there were those who called blogs "the samizdat of the 21st century" – a reference to the underground newsletters self-published by Soviet dissidents during the Cold War. And, for a time, bloggers and independent journalists did do some astounding work in places like Russia, China, Iran, Cuba, Egypt and Azerbaijan.

The BBG created the Internet Anti-Censorship (or "IAC" program) to accomplish two simple goals. The first is to support journalists, bloggers, civil society actors and activists to use the Internet safely and without fear of interference. The second is empower world citizens to have access to modern communication channels that are free of restrictions, and allow them to communicate without fear of repressive censorship or surveillance.

Using funds provided by Congress for internet freedom programs, our International Broadcasting Bureau funds large scale proxy servers and other means to defeat censorship, such as proxy servers like Psiphon. Through the BBG's investment and supports of multiple circumvention technologies, we have been able to create a new generation of mobile apps that directly challenge and overcome the firewall of Iran and Great Firewall of China. Our web proxy servers allow literally over a billion sessions a day of Internet users from the Middle East, North Africa, Eurasia and East Asia to access news and information outside of their tightly controlled information markets.

Through our Open Technology Fund, we underwrite apps and programs for computers and mobile devices that help to encrypt communications and evade censorship. OTF's approach to identify and support next-generation internet freedom technologies has led to the development of first-of-its kind tools which support encryption of text messages and mobile phone calls, detection of mobile phone censorship and intrusion efforts, and technologies which allow transfer of data without use of the internet or mobile networks. Such efforts allow users facing changing methods of curtailing free expression online to continue to communicate safely.

The success of our Internet Freedom work is at the core of our role as journalists and reflects our unique capabilities within the U.S. government. In the digital era, the freedom to speak and the freedom to listen remain essential. And you can count on the BBG expanding our efforts in this area into the future.

Cooperation between BBG and Department of Defense

Finally, I would like to turn towards our engagement with other U.S. government colleagues. The BBG has a unique set of capabilities that were enabled by a range of authorities and requirements that first established and then grew U.S. international media. While we do work closely with other parts of government to accomplish our own mission, the Board of Governors and staff at the BBG remain committed to, and strong guardians of, the Agency's statutory journalistic firewall, which ensures the independence and journalistic integrity of our broadcasts and other content.

Having said this, the BBG does cooperate effectively with other U.S. government agencies, including colleagues at the Department of Defense, Department of State, USAID, and the Centers for Disease Control. We have a number of projects already underway with each agency, and are exploring others where appropriate.

The BBG has worked closely with various different DoD commands to accomplish mutual goals. In an agreement with Africa Command, the Voice of America produced a youth program to understand the impacts of violent extremism among Somalia youth. The radio programming was supplemented by SMS messaging, Town Hall meetings and journalism training for young people.

In Southeast Asia we have executed an agreement with Pacific Command that enabled the BBG to launch a new journalism effort focused on extremism in that region, including Thailand, Indonesia, Bangladesh and Malaysia.

And Voice of America continues to train broadcast technicians and photographers within the combatant commands in the technical aspects of journalism. We are already laying plans to host and train more technical operations staff during the FY 2016 fiscal year.

Conclusion

To close, the fundamental purpose and intent of the BBG is to empower our audiences to own their future. We enable this goal by providing fact-based alternatives to the propaganda they suffer, giving them access to truth, and demonstrating the building blocks of democratic society – accountability, rule of law (versus rule by law), human security issues, and more.
Voice of America's first broadcast stated: "The news may be good or bad; we will tell you the truth." At BBG, we continue to operate with that in mind, because truth builds trust and credibility, and delivering credible news is the most effective means to ensure impact and provide the audience with information that will affect their daily lives and use in their own decision-making.

60 Years Israel Navy
(Chel ha'Yam ha'Yisraeli)

By Klaus Mommsen

Much has been written about Israel's army and air force, but modern historians largely ignore the Israeli navy. *60 Years Israel Navy* fills the void. Author Klaus Mommsen, a retired Captain in German naval intelligence, presents a thoroughly researched but highly readable portrait of the Chel Ha'yam from its inception through the early 21st Century.

Organized chronologically, the book covers all aspects of the Israeli navy's history, including equipment, operations, organizational development, and distinguished personnel. Naval commando operations feature prominently throughout, as do coup de main strikes by Israeli warships on enemy naval bases. Mommsen also thoroughly depicts how the roles and missions of the Chel Ha'yam have repeatedly changed over the last sixty years, and discusses the decades-long debate between advocates of a coastal defense & commando-oriented navy versus proponents of high-seas operations.

Another highlight is Mommsen's narrative regarding the Israeli navy's covert foreign operations to procure ships and equipment in circumvention of embargos.

Given the unresolved tensions in the Middle East, any narrative of Israeli military history runs the risk of becoming politicized. Mommsen has successfully avoided these shoals. He provides a thoroughly balanced presentation without "political correctness", but with an audible nod of respect for the Chel Ha'yam's notable achievements under the most difficult circumstances.

60 Years Israel Navy is a superb addition to the literature on modern Israeli and Middle Eastern military history. Naval and military professionals, scholars, and libraries should add this volume to their bookshelves.

Notice: 60 Years Israeli Navy is not published by Transatlantic Euro-American Multimedia LLC. This is a review of a book marketed by an external publisher.

Seizing the Strategic Narrative

Enders Wimbush

I am honored to have this opportunity to speak candidly to you about the challenges to and opportunities for U.S. international broadcasting, issues with which I have been intimately involved for my entire professional life. In the 1980s, I had the privilege of advising then Radio Free Europe/Radio Liberty president James Buckley on strategies for broadcasting to Eastern Europe and the Soviet Union. In 1987, I became Director of Radio Liberty, and I held that post during tumultuous years featuring the fall of the Berlin Wall and the collapse of the USSR. In 2010, I was nominated to the Broadcasting Board of Governors (BBG), where I served for two years. I believe that I am the only BBG governor ever to have actually directed the operations of a U.S. international broadcasting network.

I recount this brief biography to demonstrate that my perspective on the issues before you is long, detailed, and steeped in both US international broadcasting's operational details, in its history of successes and failures, and in strategies for connecting U.S. international broadcasting to the objectives of American foreign policy. In my short remarks today, I wish to focus on three key issues. First, I will address the new media environment and the challenges to US international broadcasting today. Second, I will discuss as briefly as possible the reasons the BBG cannot meet these challenges adequately, although this subject warrants a very long discussion. And third, I will address the proposed HR 2323 legislation before you, attempting to link its provisions to these other issues.

First, today's media environment.

Two facts are critical for understanding the shape and dynamics of this environment, while revealing the challenge to US international broadcasting in finding a niche within it. The first fact should be self-evident. In contrast to the period of the Cold War in which our adversaries for the most part successfully monopolized sources of information available to their populations, no such monopolization is possible today, except in a very few places. Very few countries such as North Korea exist in which governments control and approve all the information. To the contrary, a casual drive across Central Asia, Russia, the Middle East, Africa, and most of Asia reveals a sustained explosion of information sources available to these populations. Apartment balconies in cities routinely boast one satellite dish and often as many as three. Rural communities, likewise, are similarly empowered most places, and I have even seen satellite dishes on shepherds' huts in parts of the Middle East and in the Caucasus. It is no exaggeration to suggest that these people routinely receive several hundred channels of something.

The second fact is that our adversaries in have raised the quality of their media game significantly. For the most part, gone are the big lies; in are nuanced explanations for why these actors have behaved as they have. Sometimes these actors attempt the big lie, but these usually fail precisely because so many other sources of information are available to contradict them. Instead, they try to control the information that matters to them; that is, less control over the visible facts, and more over the context. They seek to explain, to obfuscate, through filters of their own interests why these facts are important, what they mean in the context their own interests, how they contribute to historical justifications for particular actions, and why they are consistent with their identities, what they seek to achieve, and their visions of the future. Networks like Russia Today (RT), China's CCTV, and the Middle East's Al Jazeera have large followings, including increasingly in the United States where all broadcast. Their power is not that they can claim different sets of facts, but in their interpretation of facts in evidence. In a word, context. And their strategies for adjusting the context to resonate with different audiences shows growing sophistication. *The New York Times* claims to purvey "all the news that's fit to print," and Fox News bills itself as "fair and balanced." RT, CCTV, and Al Jazeera, among others, make similar claims for themselves, and many people believe them.

If most of the world is awash in information, and the competition is less over facts than over context, then the appropriate niche in this media landscape for U.S. international broadcasting should be to provide deep, well resourced, and factually accurate context. The "America" piece should be central to this context. Foreign audiences crave to know how Americans think about things, and the spectrum of different opinions that inform our worldview. In particular, they want to know how our policy is made, and how the policy process reflects our worldview and the different opinions comprised within it. And they seek to understand the impact of our values on our policies and our visions. They want to know who we are, what we believe, and how we are likely to behave, even when they dislike us.

If U.S. international broadcasting has only one reason to exist it should be to seize the strategic narrative about ourselves: to convey an unvarnished version of who Americans are, what we believe and why, and what we hope to accomplish with our policies. This task properly falls to the Voice of America. As an expert on the Middle East told me recently: "Tell our story!... We are not going to stop people from hating America if they choose to hate it, but let them hate what exists, not some figment of their imagination." If you wish to know about America, U.S. international broadcasting should be your first stop. This is fundamental, because our adversaries' propaganda centers on distorting America's story in ways that serve their interests.

The Voice of America Charter is explicit on this point. The network's product must be "a consistently reliable and authoritative source of news … objective, accurate, and comprehensive." But it must also "represent America" by presenting "a balanced and comprehensive projection of significant American thought and institutions," while articulating its policies "clearly and effectively," as well as "responsible discussions and opinions on these policies." This is not to say that the VOA speaks for the U.S.

government. Indeed, it does not. But it should have a point of view that reflects our values. And this point of view is, or should be, its vital essence.

Some thoughts on the Broadcasting Board of Governors. In my view, the BBG was poorly conceived in the beginning, and, not surprisingly, it has performed poorly. One need not take my word for it; the frequent and on-going evaluations, Office of Inspector General (OIG) reports, independent audits, and informed analyses are unremittingly negative and critical. Criticisms fall into several categories:

- Dysfunction. This is well known and well documented in a host of reports from the OIG. A comprehensive report of January 2013, for example, highlights problems in individual board member conduct, nepotism, backsliding on strategy, ethics, and travel expenses, among other things. https://oig.state.gov/system/files/203193.pdf

  Lack of oversight. A June 2015 report from the OIG cites Radio Free Asia for dodgy expenditures, possible conflicts of interest and other matters. https://oig.state.gov/system/files/aud-fm-ib-15-24.pdf The BBG is criticized for lacking "a well-defined structure to monitor grantee activities." A November 2014 independent audit identifies BBG's weak "control environment" that has led to its inability to effectively monitor its grantees. https://oig.state.gov/system/files/aud-fm-ib-15-10.pdf

- Lack of strategy. A July 2015 OIG inspection of VOA and RFE/RL operations in Kabul noted that "specific strategies for harmonizing the operations in Afghanistan have lingered for 10 years without specific implementation actions." https://oig.state.gov/system/files/isp-ib-15-32.pdf A September 2013 inspection of BBG operations in Moscow called for "a comprehensive strategy for U.S. international broadcasting to Russia that includes all Broadcasting Board of Governors entities operating in or broadcasting to Russia." https://oig.state.gov/system/files/217908.pdf

A current on-going investigation of possible financial and oversight malfeasance at RFE/RL in Prague, occurring from at least 2013 to the present, which has gained the attention of the OIG, the FBI, and possibly other federal authorities, is probably a low-point in BBG oversight, given that the BBG board knew of the problem at least a year before it acted, and then only weakly. This is a pretty miserable record for such a small agency, which also consistently receives one of the worst rankings in surveys of federal employees' satisfaction with their place of work.

The BBG suffers from serious structural deficiencies, many inherited from earlier times but still unaddressed, an unremarkable observation that the BBG apparently recognized in its own "Strategic Plan," recently posted on its website, almost certainly in response to the proposed legislation. The BBG wildly duplicates capabilities across the five networks at great expense to the taxpayer and to little effect. By my count, of the 61 language services hosted by the five BBG networks 22 are duplicated—that is, more than one third. In practical terms, this means that U.S. international broadcasting has two separate broadcast services in Albanian, Azerbaijani, Dari, Pashto, Armenian, Bosnian, Georgian, Persian, Macedonian, Russian, Serbian, Ukrainian, Uzbek, Burmese, Cantonese, Khmer, Korean, Lao, Mandarin, Tibetan, Vietnamese, and Spanish.

So many duplicate services spread across different networks creates a number of problems. Duplicating services and operational support systems costs lots of money, and it also has severe negative implications for mission effectiveness and oversight. Taxpayers deserve better stewardship of their money.

Next, the strategic problem. Funding duplication severely limits the ability of U.S. international broadcasting to fund new languages when it would benefit our foreign policy, or to double down on critical languages that might help us shape a rapidly changing environment. Spreading these surrogate broadcasters out across multiple network structures dilutes both their impact and any effort to develop a strategic critical mass.

Third, the operational problem. No one—and I mean literally no one—really knows how these services are duplicating, where they contradict one another (or U. S policy), and where their efforts might be made to converge to create something larger than the sum of their parts. Efforts over many years—indeed, over several decades—to force a modicum of common purpose between the duplicates at VOA, RFE/RL, and Radio Free Asia have been described by different BBGs as "complementary," "cooperation," "harmonization," or—the most innovative effort to justify this waste as something useful—"parallax." "Parallax" is described by one of my colleagues as choosing to own two leaking barns over one solid structure.

The BBG board has also failed to deal with chronic leadership issues. When the board I served on took office in 2010, we almost immediately voted to install a CEO to deal with issues that cross network boundaries. It took five full years for the board to appoint a true CEO, and he left after 42 days. A new CEO has now been appointed—and I wish him well—but it is unclear if he has the authority or support to make the tough decisions required to force asset sharing across networks, end duplication, replace poor leaders and hire new ones, create the processes to allow programming to respond rapidly to changing conditions in the broadcast environment, or harness the most effective technologies to the task.

The leadership issue goes top to bottom in U.S. international broadcasting. Kevin Klose, sitting next to me, was the last full-fledged president of RFE/RL. He left 19 months ago, on March 1, 2014, leaving that vital network—now in probably the most challenging environment since the end of the Cold War—under the control of two "acting interim co-managers"—one located in Washington, who has since departed. RFE/RL still has no permanent president, even as its broadcast milieu churns. The VOA has had no director for nearly eight months. The management of the BBG itself, lacking a CEO or any other credible arrangement, was handed to the joint leadership of three executives, two of whom could be described as junior. The leadership problem is epidemic.

Most concerning, the BBG is allergic to strategy, which is another way of saying that it is mostly unhinged from the processes and practice of US foreign policy for which it was intended. This is the case because BBG's governance is weak. The board on which I served advanced a strong and comprehensive reform plan within weeks of taking office, most of whose key elements are now included in HR 2323. Our plan was voted into effect unanimously by that board. Then it was almost immediately sabotaged by two members of the board who adopted opposing agendas. In the end, virtually none of it was implemented. The debate over most of its elements continues with the current board, which is no closer than we were to bringing real change to U.S. international broadcasting.

Ukraine posed a particularly tough test for the BBG. The BBG's response to Ukraine has been neither robust nor quick, despite an influx of new taxpayer funds for the purpose. Nearly a year and a half after Russia invaded the Crimea thereby touching off today's crisis in Ukraine, the BBG was able to produce a single half-hour of new daily programming for placement on local networks in Central Europe, and then only by mostly working around the existing capabilities in the two Russian broadcast services in RFE/RL and the VOA and with an infusion of an additional million dollars from the State Department. Is the BBG telling us this is the best we can do? Clearly it is a feeble response. I am told that the quality of the product is quite good, though it often airs late at night on local networks, and that new programs are now being added. But the BBG's response to Ukraine leaves much to be desired.

Strategy at the BBG tends to be driven by the budget. For example, every year I spent on the board I had to defend the tiny expenditure for Tatar-Bashkir broadcasts. The cost of Tatar-Bashir broadcasts is not much more than a rounding error in the overall BBG budget, but this is exactly what makes it vulnerable to cutting when budgets get tight and economies are necessary. The Tatar-Bashkir regions of Russia sit at the epicenter of its historic Islamic populations, which are in danger of radicalization like other parts of the Islamic world. When Russia's spiral of instability accelerates, as it will, America will eventually wish to communicate to Tatars and Bashkirs as a strategic imperative. The same fate nearly claimed the North Caucasus service, which broadcasts to an area of growing radicalization, for the same reason. Meanwhile, the VOA's impressive English language broadcasts have repeatedly faced severe cuts or elimination, despite being a principal language of young elites around the globe. The budget should not drive these important strategic decisions.

It is worrisome that any discussion of strategy nearly always defaults to questions of technology, the operative question being: Which technologies allow us to deliver our broadcasts effectively to our audiences? This is easy, because one can bring in experts from Silicon Valley and elsewhere to discuss new social media and digital communications more generally without really having to get into the weeds about what it is strategically we seek to accomplish or local limitations to particular technologies. Technology should be part of strategy, but it is not strategy by itself. Largely absent are serious discussions by experts about content, audience, and impact: What should we be broadcasting, to whom, and to what end? What audiences do we seek to influence? How should we measure impact? Do numbers matter? And how does all of this contribute to advancing our foreign policy objectives? These are difficult issues for any BBG, whose members often lack strong foreign policy experience and dynamics in the broadcast environment. Almost none have had much experience with international broadcasting of this kind.

Adding a new CEO to this mix—and investing him or her with authority to determine "strategy"—will not begin to answer this problem. Strategy is a key responsibility of the board, not the CEO. Yet we have already been alerted that the BBG's new CEO will address a meeting of the U.S. Advisory Commission on Public Diplomacy on December 2nd to discuss "The BBG's New Strategic Direction." What is this new strategy and how was it arrived at? This seems somewhat premature for someone holding this post for a only few weeks.

Finally, a few words on the proposed HR 2323. Former BBG Governor Dennis Mulhaupt and I in July of last year addressed the state of U.S. international broadcasting and the need to reform it radically. Little has changed since then in either its condition or the urgency to reform it. in. http://www.weeklystandard.com/blogs/fixing-us-international-broadcasting-last_796034.html?page=2

I am a strong proponent of this legislation. It needs a few adjustments, in my view, that will make it even stronger and more effective. In my discussions with the SFRC staff, I know they are aware of most of my concerns and those of my colleagues who also support reform. But I urge the committee to move rapidly on this legislation, and to be bold. The reform that created the BBG and the current structure failed early and, I would argue, quite spectacularly. This should not be repeated.

The proposed legislation accomplishes a number of essential things, as

First, it "reaffirms the important safeguards enshrined in the VOA charter," but insists that the VOA serve as America's voice. The "America piece," so vital to our strategic narrative and for making our values, visions, and policies understood around the globe, will no longer be discounted or ignored.

Second, the surrogate networks—Radio Free Europe/Radio Liberty, Radio Free Asia, the Middle East Broadcast Networks, and, one hopes, the Office of Cuban Broadcasting— will enjoy priority and urgency in implementing a historic mission that requires comprehensive strategy to support America's interests in a vastly more complex political environment. They will benefit specifically from being liberated from the BBG structure and the provision of their own private and dedicated board. This independence is essential for the surrogates to meet new challenges squarely and expertly.

Third, creating what amounts to two companies from five should engender significant savings and asset sharing, while encouraging more mission-centric strategic focus.

Fourth, the proposed oversight structures will be more specialized and defined, closer to the audiences they seek to influence, and management will be more accountable to them. Board members with expert knowledge of our broadcast regions—especially with respect to the proposed Consolidated Grantees—should promote a much closer connection between U.S. international broadcasting and our foreign policy objectives.

Project 1704:

A U.S. Army War College Analysis of Russian Strategy in Eastern Europe, an Appropriate U.S. Response, and the Implications for U.S. Landpower

The strategic calculus changed in Europe with the 2014 Russian seizure of Crimea and its ongoing war against Ukraine. Compounding the dilemma of an aggressive Russia, is the application of ambiguity to create a clock of uncertainty that prevents a decisive response to counter its destabilizing activities. However, this application of ambiguity is easily defeated, if nations are willing to take concerted efforts now to preempt and deter further Russian aggression. Project 1704 provides an honest assessment of the tenuous strategic environment that now envelopes Eastern Europe and offers specific recommendations on how to continue the 70 years of unparalleled peace that most of Europe has enjoyed.

To order please visit www.teamultimedia.com

Engage and Connect:
Global Journalism Serving America

Jeff Shell

Jeff Shell is Chairman of the Broadcasting Board of Governors. He provided these insights into BBG reform before the Senate Foreign Relations Committee on November 17, 2015.

Chairman Corker, Ranking Member Cardin, and Members of the Committee, thank you for inviting me to speak to the unique role that the Broadcasting Board of Governors (BBG) and United States international media play in advancing our national interests.

I am pleased to be joined today by my colleagues Governor Ken Weinstein and CEO John Lansing. Alongside the rest of the Board and staff at the International Broadcasting Bureau and across the BBG, we are working diligently to shape the Broadcasting Board of Governors into a unique and powerful tool in the U.S. foreign policy toolkit. The BBG team deserves a lot of credit for their consistently excellent programming and I want to use this opportunity to thank them.

Let me also thank the Members of this Committee for shining a light on the important work that the Broadcasting Board of Governors carries out on behalf of the United States. Many Americans are not aware of Broadcasting Board of Governors, its unique mission and growing role in international media.

Put simply, our job at BBG is "to inform, engage, and connect people around the world in support of freedom and democracy." To do so, we oversee all nonmilitary international broadcasting supported by the U.S. government, including the Voice of America (VOA), the Office of Cuba Broadcasting (OCB), and BBG-funded grantees Radio Free Europe/Radio Liberty (RFE/RL), Radio Free Asia (RFA) and the Middle East Broadcasting Networks (MBN).

We use these resources to provide news and information to overseas audiences that lack adequate sources of objectives news and information about their countries and societies, their region, the United States, and the world. In short, we put fact-based journalism to work, on a global scale, on behalf of the American people.

Our reach is global. BBG radio, television, Internet, and mobile programs are consumed by more than 226 million people each week, in more than 100 countries in sixty-one languages – many of them in communities and countries that face organized misinformation campaigns.

Global media is an area that I understand well. As Chairman of Universal Filmed Entertainment Group, my day job, I oversee worldwide operations for Universal Pictures. And prior to taking on my current role, I served as Chairman of NBCUniversal International in London, where I was responsible for overseeing the operations of all NBCUniversal International businesses, and as President of Comcast Programming Group.

In my professional experience, international media is marked by complexity. In my current job it is my responsibility to ensure that Universal's programming remains successful in a rapidly changing global media environment. I note similar challenges through my role at the BBG, where we not only must contend with a dynamic media landscape but also the asymmetric challenge of state and non-state actors, often well-funded, who effectively deploy media and digital tools to challenge the United States, our values of democracy and freedom, and the very existence of objective truth.

It is critical to acknowledge that in the recent past the BBG has not responded as effectively as it could to these growing challenges. As with any media organization, be it Universal Pictures or the BBG, the responsibility for organizational breakdown and inertia starts at the top. Some of our past problems derived from Board dysfunction and the failure to link the work of the Board to the day-to-day operations of the BBG's global team, and the growing sense of irrelevance and inability to "join the fight" that these challenges engendered.

But despite past challenges, two facts remained enduring. First, the BBG's mission remained unassailably critical to U.S. foreign policy. Second, we boast a team of brave and hardworking individuals who work around the world, in relative obscurity and often outright danger, each and every day to fulfill the BBG's mission to inform, engage, and connect people around the world in support of freedom and democracy.

These facts informed the work of the Board as we sought to overcome past challenges and ensure the meaningful impact of BBG efforts across the globe. I am happy to report that we are making significant progress on this front.

Our biggest change is that our current Board is fully united behind the changes we need to make to ensure BBG's success, and the ways we need to operate to do so. We are non-partisan and comprised of media and foreign affairs experts who deeply believe in the BBG mission and the need to lead the U.S.' fight against the "weaponization of information" by our adversaries and challengers. The level of cooperation and expertise on this Board is the best I have seen, be it inside government or outside.

Most importantly, we recognize that the Board's role cannot be operational. The BBG is a complex institution and it is beyond the ability of any appointed Board, comprised of appointees with day jobs, to manage it effectively. Recognizing this fact, the Board elected to shift all the powers it could legally delegate to a Chief Executive Officer, who would oversee all aspects of U.S. international media and provide day-to-day management of BBG operations.

A critical act in this regard was to select John Lansing to serve our CEO. John's experience and temperament make him the perfect person for this job. He is a recognized leader in media management, having served nine years as President of Scripps Networks, where he is credited with guiding the company to become a leading developer of unique content across various media platforms including television, digital, mobile and publishing. Equally important, he is a journalist at heart – formerly an award-winning photojournalist and field producer, assignment manager, managing editor, and news director at multiple television stations earlier in his career.

And we have taken steps to modernize our operations as well. For instance, in 2014, we undertook a comprehensive review of the efficacy of shortwave radio as a distribution platform for U.S. international media, which resulted in a shift in focus to digital and mobile tools as our future tools of choice, because that is where our audiences are now and where they will be in the future. CEO Lansing will address our aggressive shift to digital media in his testimony.

Additionally, the BBG is embracing new tools to support the fundamental right of information freedom. Through the Internet Anti-Censorship Program and Open Technology Fund, we are supporting journalists, bloggers, civil society actors, and activists to use the Internet safely and without fear of interference.

Finally, through the strong presence on the Board of Under Secretary of State for Public Diplomacy and Public Affairs Richard Stengel, we are more coordinated with the Department of State than ever before. Closer coordination has allowed the BBG to use its unique resources to impact in some of today's most important foreign policy arenas, such as on the digital battlefield in Ukraine or the global threat of violent extremism.

We recognize we also need to be better coordinated with Congress, which is why we are deeply appreciative of the opportunity to speak to this Committee today. In taking the above listed steps, and many others, the current Board has demonstrated its clear commitment to positioning BBG to succeed in the modern media environment. We look to Congress to provide certain additional authorities that will further ensure our success.

First, and foremost, we need the Congress fully enshrine the CEO as the operational lead at BBG. While the Board has elected to delegate key powers to the CEO through its own volition, it is clear that we need to institutionalize this role through legislation so that all future Boards can benefit from expert operational leadership.

Furthermore, we not only need to enshrine the role of the CEO, but we also need to fully empower the position to serve all relevant functions as required by the Board. As I mentioned previously, the sitting Board elected to delegate all authorities that it legally could to the CEO – but unfortunately the Board lacks the authority to fully modernize in this regard. We require legislation to authorize the Board to delegate the remainder of its authorities, required for effective and efficient day-to- day operation of the agency, to the CEO, so that the Board may focus on strategic oversight and governance.

This includes the currently "non-delegable" authority of the Board to reallocate even the most *de minimis* dollar amount of funds across the various bureaus and federal and grantee broadcasting entities of the BBG when requirements change. In other words, in order to move even one penny between the entities, even under the most urgent of circumstances, the CEO must seek a vote of the full Board.

Beyond these management fixes, we also need to ensure further structural and operational agility, if we are to successfully counter today's dynamic challenges in the information space. Unfortunately, many of our existing authorities, a number of which date back to 1948, or thereabouts, are either obsolete or incomplete for our purposes as a 21st century organization.

A key area in this regard is surge capacity. When crises arise, BBG is often asked to surge its efforts to the affected region quickly. The International Broadcasting Act requires the agency to do so by providing for "the capability to provide a surge capacity to support United States foreign policy objectives during crises abroad." But, as a surge generally requires increased content and broadcasting, we require not just enhanced authority to operate notwithstanding certain standard processes, but also the ability to turn to a ready source of funding. For us, this means the authority to receive or fully utilize funds from other agencies, or to make use of a no-year fund established for this purpose.

With these fixes, the BBG will be best positioned to thrive in its mandated role as a unique tool in the U.S. foreign affairs toolbox, and will be a powerful force for countering the challenges posed by the growth of misleading or propagandistic information globally.

Mr. Chairman, I would like to conclude on a more personal note. As Chairman of Universal Filmed Entertainment Group, I have been lucky enough to lead an organization that has secured its most profitable and successful years in memory. We released films such as "Jurassic World," "Furious 7," and "Straight Outta Compton" to critical acclaim and commercial success. I am immensely proud of that success. But that pride at these successes pales in comparison to how proud I am to serve my country as Chairman of the Broadcasting Board of Governors, and the incredible progress we have made over the past two years on behalf of the American people. I look forward to working with the Congress, and this Committee, on our work still to come.

Russian Political, Economic, and Security Issues and U.S. Interests

By Jim Nichol

Discusses Russian-American relations since the end of the Soviet Union, including US economic aid to Russia. Discusses US efforts to influence political and economic reform in post-Soviet Russia, and bilateral cooperation on such issues as terrorism and proliferation. Analyzes the deterioration of US-Russia relations since the 2008 Russian invasion of Georgia, and escalating bilateral tensions since 2012, up to and including the current occupation of the Crimea and threats against Ukraine. Discusses America's practical interests in US-Russian cooperation, and explores the reasons behind the deterioration of relations since the accession of Vladimir Putin despite Barack Obama's attempts to "reset" US-Russian relations.

To order please visit www.teamultimedia.com

U.S. International Broadcasting
for the 21st Century

John Lansing

John Lansing is CEO and Director of the Broadcasting Board of Governors. He provided this assessment before the Senate Foreign Relations Committee on November 17, 2015.

Chairman Corker, Ranking Member Cardin, and Members of the Committee, thank you for inviting me to speak today regarding the future of the Broadcasting Board of Governors (BBG) and United States international media. I am pleased to join BBG Chairman Jeff Shell and BBG Governor Ken Weinstein today.

I currently serve as the Chief Executive Officer and Director of the BBG, where I oversee all operational aspects of U.S. international media and provide day-to-day management of BBG networks on behalf of the Board.

In my testimony today I want to present my initial reactions to the BBG mission, detail our effectiveness, and outline some of the steps I am taking to position the BBG to be both a leader in the international media space and a uniquely powerful tool in the U.S. foreign policy toolbox.

Prior to my current role as BBG CEO, I served for nine years as President of Scripps Networks, where I helped the company become a leading developer of unique content across various media platforms including television, digital, mobile and publishing.

More important, I am a journalist at heart. I started out as a photojournalist in the field, with a camera on my shoulder, and from there I was hooked. I worked my way up to serve as a field producer, assignment manager, managing editor, and news director at television stations in Detroit, Michigan and Cleveland, Ohio.

It is through my professional experience as a journalist that I gained deep respect for the vital role that impartial, fact-based reporting plays in our society. By holding people, institutions, and governments accountable to the truth – and by arming citizens with undeniable facts – journalists show, often indirectly and subtly, how democracies should work. Great journalism presents not only the news, but also the context of that news to provide audiences with a greater understanding of their world and to empower them to take action.

As President Obama said in his speech at the 2015 U.N. General Assembly: "The strength of nations depends on the success of their people – their knowledge, their innovation, their imagination, their creativity, their drive, their opportunity – and that, in turn, depends upon individual rights and good governance and personal security."

The Broadcasting Board of Governors is fundamentally engaged in the business of fact-based journalism. We are not a propaganda outfit. Rather, we advance U.S. national interests by engaging audiences that are critical to furthering democratic values through open and free exchanges of information.

Throughout U.S. international media's long history, the tools and goals have been unwavering: to deliver consistently accurate, reliable and credible reporting that opens minds and stimulates debate in closed societies and those where free media are not yet fully established – especially where local media fails to inform and empower its citizens.

In short, we inform, engage, and connect people around the world in support of freedom and democracy. This mission is critically important because, more than ever before, information matters.

In today's increasingly interconnected world, responding to the global explosion of information must no longer be considered as a "value added" function in support of broader strategic ends, but rather a key focus of U.S. foreign policy in its own right. Today's media has the power to reach through the screen to activate audiences to action – or to suppress them. Failing to recognize this fact limits the effectiveness of our foreign policy.

Our global agenda will not be effective if we fail to appreciate how the flow of information shapes the actions of policymakers, institutions, and everyday citizens on the street, and capitalize on these trends.

Equally important, we must constantly evaluate how audiences' media consumption preferences change – and we must change with them – if we are to be successful. Any media executive worth his or her salt understands that as markets and audiences evolve, so too must your organization if it is to remain competitive and impactful.

As CEO of the BBG, I recognize that we must change as well. Chairman Shell outlined a few solutions that we believe the Congress can provide that would allow the BBG to succeed in the 21st Century. First and foremost, we need legislation to enshrine a Chief Executive Officer position at the BBG who is empowered to manage all BBG operations and functions, including the ability to shift resources as needed and appoint senior officials.

But, regardless of these legislative fixes, my team and I have taken action internally to move the BBG into a more modern, impactful stance. As our adversaries have embraced the opportunities to engage and influence audiences using new tools and techniques, so too must the BBG team.

The key driver of all of our internal reforms is *impact*. Our success no longer depends on our unique global reach, but also on the intensity of the BBG's relationships with its audiences, the extent to which they share and comment on our news and information and, ultimately, how they influence local knowledge and thought.

The impact of U.S. international media for the next decade will be based on our ability to be an influential news and information source in this dynamic 21st century information environment. We cannot afford to lose our status as a global, influential news service. BBG's programming must exist on the platforms our audiences prefer and use. It must include content that moves and engages them. It must include a focus on regions of the world that need us the most –closed or closing societies. It must use modern tools to embrace younger demographics and engage them as future influencers.

In order to accomplish these imperatives, I, with the unanimous support of the Board, am aggressively prioritizing five core themes to ensure the BBG is the 21st century media organization that the tax payers demand. I will briefly outline these themes here, but I am happy to answer any questions, and brief you in greater detail on any of these points, as needed.

First, we are accelerating our shift toward engaging audiences on digital platforms, especially utilizing the power of video, mobile, and social networks. If we are to be a credible information source we must be on the platforms used by our audiences – be it radio and television, or mobile tools and social media. These platforms not only reach new audiences, but represent a shift from one-way dissemination, to more empowering and engaging audience participation.

A great example of this ethos is the Middle East Broadcasting Networks' (MBN) "Raise Your Voice" campaign, which encourages citizens across the Middle East to speak out and be a part of the discussion about the fight against violent extremism. Over just the past four months more than 590,000 votes have been cast on daily "Raise Your Voice" polls and MBN now has 12.3 million followers on Facebook.

Second, we are rapidly expanding coordination and content-sharing across the BBG's five interdependent networks in order to cover and report on the stories that matter to audiences and markets that increasingly transcend political borders and languages. For instance, this will allow us to more effectively share our unique coverage of the Middle East with interested audiences in Indonesia and Russia, or issues surrounding Chinese investment in Africa with audiences across Latin America.

BBG has taken several notable steps in this regard already. One of my first steps as CEO was to convene the U.S. International Media Coordinating Council (ICC), comprised of the heads of each of our five networks.

The BBG's five networks – Voice of America, the Office of Cuba Broadcasting, Radio Free Europe/Radio Liberty, Radio Free Asia and the Middle East Broadcasting Networks – operate independently and effectively. But, in many instances, they may have overlapping stakes on key stories – for example, violent extremism or Russian military action in Syria.

In order to better coordinate our reporting, and make use of scarce resources, the ICC now meets monthly to discuss ongoing reporting, share information, and join forces where possible on hard-hitting reporting.

Voice of America (VOA) and Radio Free Europe/Radio Liberty (RFE/RL) are already making powerful strides on this front. The two networks worked together to create *Current Time,* a popular daily 30-minute Russian-language television news program that is now available in nine European countries of the former Soviet Union via 25 media outlets, and worldwide via digital platforms. In Russia, where placement on domestic stations is not possible, *Current Time* is available on NewsTube.ru, Russia's largest news site. Our new research shows that nearly two million people in Russia are watching *Current Time* weekly online and that the program is most popular among 15-24 year olds.

Third, the BBG is concentrating its efforts in five key issue areas where we can be most effective in support of our mission. While our reach is global, the BBG cannot cover all events with equal intensity; we need to focus our efforts.

To do so, we are focusing our reporting on the key spheres of importance that matter most to U.S. foreign policy, U.S. global interests, and the U.S. taxpayer:

- Reporting on Russia;
- Covering violent extremism;
- The widening regional influence of Iran;
- China, not only in the South China Sea region, but also in Africa and Latin America;
- Promoting universal rights and fundamental freedoms in Cuba.

Fourth, we are evolving to an organization actively engaged in curating, commissioning, and acquiring content. For broader impact, we need to focus BBG original reporting to not just rehash the daily news, but to provide depth and perspective on events for more meaning and impact. To do so, we will complement our deeper original reporting through the added curation of external content.

Curating external content will not only free up BBG resources for more impactful, in-depth reporting, it will also potentially support the new generations of compelling storytellers, such as the youth in many of our markets, documentarians and journalists that engage their peers every day on digital platforms.

Finally, we are emphasizing impact over sheer reach. In the past, the BBG was asked to focus primarily on maximizing the number of people our programs potentially reached. This number-centric strategy was befitting a broadcasting organization with a broadcasting mentality. But in today's digital and engaged media environment, we must focus on more than just reach. By putting the audience first in how we collect, create and distribute news and information, we take a more modern approach to informing, engaging and connecting with our audiences.

These five priorities provide an initial framework for how the BBG will position itself as an influential media source on the global stage, and as a more functional tool in the USG strategic toolkit. I look forward to working with this Committee, and the rest of the Congress, to implement these strategies fully.

To close, the fundamental purpose and intent of the BBG is to empower our audiences to own their future. We do this by providing fact-based alternatives to the propaganda, offering them access to truth, and demonstrating the building blocks of democratic society – accountability, rule of law (versus rule by law), human security, and more.

Voice of America's first broadcast stated: "The news may be good or bad; we will tell you the truth." At BBG, we continue to operate with that mindset, because truth builds trust and credibility, and delivering credible news is the most effective means to ensure impact and provide the audience with information that will affect their daily lives and empower their own decision-making.

Countering Disinformation
With Information:
Defeating Adversary Propaganda to
Win Hearts and Minds

Kenneth R. Weinstein

Kenneth R. Weinstein is President and CEO of the Hudson Institute. He presented this analysis before the Senate Foreign Relations Committee on November 17, 2015.

Chairman Corker, Ranking Member Cardin, and Members of the Committee, thank you for inviting me to speak today on the impact that the Broadcasting Board of Governors (BBG) and United States international media has around the world. We as a nation need to remain vigilant to the ways in which information and ideas, as well as disinformation and false ideologies, affect our national security, and I thank the Committee for holding today's hearing. I am pleased to join my colleagues, BBG Chairman Jeff Shell and CEO John Lansing, at today's hearing.

I have served as a Board Member on the Broadcasting Board of Governors since October 2013 and as the President and CEO of the Hudson Institute since March 2011. As a political theorist who has spent the past few decades working on U.S. foreign policy and its impact in Asia, the Middle East and Europe, I have had the opportunity to analyze the strategic context, direction, and efficacy of both U.S. foreign policy and US civilian international media.

Today, I will describe the overall operating context for BBG international media, examine some of the challenges and opportunities inherent in that context, and note important ways that BBG reporting is impacting audiences in support of U.S. foreign policy and freedom in this space.

US international media operates in an environment of rapid geopolitical change and growing instability in world affairs. Last week's horrific terror attacks in Paris are just the latest example of the challenging international environment, and one in which tragic events in one country are increasingly linked to those in others.

The broad features of recent geopolitical change include Russia's aggression in Ukraine; the spread of ISIS and other jihadist groups in the Middle East, Africa, Central Asia and now, alas, Western Europe; Iran's growing tentacles in the Middle East; economic slowdown in China, and growing assertiveness in the South China Sea.

This geopolitical instability and rising threat level occurs at a time of mass technological innovation, reducing the costs for communication to both large and targeted audiences. Across the globe, the enemies of liberty have become increasingly adept at marshaling the same cost-effective technologies that make the dissemination of information much less expensive today than it has ever been in human history.

Against this backdrop of geopolitical evolution, both elite and public opinion has proven ill-prepared about how to react to unprecedented policy change. At this time of uncertainty, state propaganda agencies have stepped into the breach, making what Peter Pomerantsev of the Legatum Institute termed the "weaponization of information" a central facet of international conflict.

The enemies of free societies – both state and non-state actors – have become increasingly skilled at "weaponization of information," aggressively using the tools of a free society, including the media and social media, to distort reality, and defend the indefensible: tyranny, kleptocracy, murder, religious intolerance and pre-modern visions of human society that deny fundamental human rights. They do so pro-actively, with creativity and attention to production value and a targeting of audiences that is far more sophisticated than the Soviet Union ever did, thereby weakening intellectual and moral opposition to their policies abroad, highlighting shortcomings of Western societies through a distorted lens, or fomenting anti- Western sentiment at home to justify inexcusable actions by their governments abroad.

Well-funded state propaganda outlets designed to have the patina of impartial media outlets include Russia's RT, Sputnik, Ruptly, Rossiya Segnodnya, and other secondary platforms, which according to State Department estimates spends over $1.4 billion annually on propaganda. The Columbia Journalism Review estimates that CCTV's English language efforts will be nineteen times the annual budget of the BBC, the world's largest news organization.

According to *The Atlantic*, al Jazeera spent $1 billion to start Al Jazeera English and the network gets $100 million for its annual budget. These differing platforms target specific audiences, especially in the West, seeking to undermine the possibility of a firm and united Western response to current policy crises.

A second major challenge the BBG faces is the transnational power of and appeal of groups such as ISIS. As predictable political borders have eroded, so have the traditional boundaries that once shaped the media landscape. Today, communities and conversations arise in a digital space without geographic limitation, and technology massively compresses the time and space needed for disinformation and influence to spread.

Social media and the Internet have proven fertile ground, not just for Russian disinformation but also for spreading Islamic radicalism, free from the more truthful filter of traditional journalism. Through social media, ISIS, itself in competition with other radical Islamist groups, projects a romanticized vision of life under the Caliphate to disaffected men and women in Western Europe, the Middle East, Africa and Asia. Teenagers in Britain, Turkey or Saudi Arabia may follow the dictates of radical Imams on YouTube and abandon the comforts of home for war-torn regions of Syria or Iraq.

These trends have important ramifications for how BBG, and others, target our intended audiences. Information-seeking communities and individuals get news updates not solely through established media outlets in limited geographical locations, but through their preferred information platforms. CEO Lansing will speak to this issue in greater detail in his testimony, so I will simply note here that moving forward we must continue to embrace digital and social media tools as key platforms for our content, as these are the tools that our priority markets – youths and future influencers – already use on a regular basis.

A second challenge is the sheer volume of available media and the effect that has on how global audiences consume information and, ultimately, make social, economic, and political decisions. Every day, global communities are awash in information. But not all information is created equal. From Crimea, to Syria, Northern Nigeria, and Southeast Asia, propaganda and censorship foment hate and confusion, monitor and suppress dissent, activate acts of terror and roll back hard- won freedoms. Actors from ISIL to China to Russia are using information not just to "win the news cycle," but to shape the very choices of statecraft.

This current context stands in stark contrast to the Cold War, during which certain global actors sought to prevent the flow of information to the point of creating vacuums in key communities, which the United States moved to fill with reporting through Voice of America, Radio Free Europe, and other tools. Today, we see the opposite: an abundance of false, doctored, or misleading information on a multitude of different platforms for consumption.

A key BBG challenge is ensuring that our high-quality reporting serves as a beacon for accurate, fact-based journalism in spaces awash with dishonest, misleading, or government-controlled information. In environments inundated with propaganda or falsehood, the best antidote is objective, fact-based reporting that arms citizens with the truth.

As such, BBG's global reach and journalistic credibility play a vital role in correcting falsehoods, holding people and institutions accountable, and demystifying U.S. policy in these communities.

Along these lines, I would like to touch on three key areas where the BBG is operating with impact in the modern media space.

Responding to Russia

The Kremlin is actively using propaganda and disinformation as a tool of foreign policy and to maintain support at home. To counter Russian propaganda, the BBG engages key audiences inside Russia, along the Russian periphery, and globally to provide them with the realities about Russian and U.S. activities and, importantly, their context. As elsewhere, we have an appreciation of different audiences that we seek to reach, and want our audiences to be empowered by facts, the most effective strategy for countering propaganda.

Since the fall of the Yanukovych government in Ukraine in February 2014, and the ensuing occupation and attempted annexation of Crimea and Russian aggression in eastern Ukraine, the BBG has dramatically increased programming to the region.
Voice of America (VOA) and Radio Free Europe/Radio Liberty (RFE/RL) have added or expanded more than 35 new programs on multiple media platforms in Russian, Ukrainian, and other languages to reach new audiences in Ukraine, Russia, elsewhere in the former Soviet space, and around the world.

U.S. International Media are a real force in Ukraine, as I have seen from my travels there. We have every reason to be proud of our journalists. We have every reason to be proud of our journalists in the field. Our coverage of the protests on the Maidan was unparalleled and our brave journalists at RFE/RL remained on the job in the face of intimidation and physical violence; their continuous and fact-based reporting of violence perpetrated by forces loyal to the Yanukovich government was critical to Ukraine's democratic revolution. Our journalists, whether at RFE/RL or Voice of America, are widely respected as among the best in the business, and our diverse programming, which at times has aired programs critical of the Poroshenko government, has broad appeal.

The BBG's response to Russian propaganda represents five broad lines of effort:

➢ Focus programming to impact strategic audiences
➢ Expand partnerships to reach audiences in local markets and influence the news agenda
➢ Move resources to digital platforms to directly engage audiences
➢ Increase research on the ground to better understand audiences and impact
➢ Utilize BBG capabilities and expertise to meet unfilled strategic needs and opportunities

The BBG is already seeing strong impact in the region. More than 500 Central Asia media outlets have already subscribed to RFE/RL's Central Asia news wire service, which launched in September in Russian and vernacular languages. Voice of America and RFE/RL programs are now carried on more than 120 television, radio and internet outlets in Ukraine.

RFE/RL continues to ramp up DIGIM, its new social-media driven digital reporting and engagement service, which includes the "Footage vs. Footage" feature, a daily video product that contrasts how Russian media and global media report on the same events, provides the facts of a case and pointing out inconsistencies and falsehoods in Russian reporting.

Additionally, RFE/RL and Voice of America have expanded *Current Time,* their popular daily 30-minute Russian-language television news program into Central Asia. It is now on the air in nine countries via 25 media outlets, and *Current Time* is available to digital audiences worldwide. In Russia, where placement on domestic stations is not possible, *Current Time* is available on NewsTube.ru, Russia's largest news site. Our new research shows that nearly two million people in Russia are watching *Current Time* weekly online, and that it is most popular among 15-24 year olds.

Through these programs we engage the audience's – often silently held – interests and concerns. Russians, for instance, are considering whether their country is heading in the right direction. They are weighing whether Putin's political and social reality is where they want to raise their children, start or grow a business, get an education; these are core questions that speak to hopes and aspirations. In other words, the future media environment is not just about countering Kremlin propaganda, but a campaign for the future of the region.

It is worth noting that the BBG is not solely engaged in reporting in this area; we also provide equipment and journalism training to key populations. For example, following consultations in June with Ukrainian authorities and our Department of State, BBG provided broadcasting transmission equipment to Ukraine to facilitate delivery of radio and television programs to audiences in areas controlled by Russia or Russian-backed separatists. The equipment: a new, 134-meter tower; a 60 kW solid state Medium Wave transmitter; and three portable FM stations, will be used as part of a low-power network to be deployed near contested areas.

Covering Violent Jihadi Movements

Extremist narratives too often go unaddressed within local media environments and digital echo chambers. These narratives are often tied to extremists' alleged religious virtue and organizational invincibility, with a toxic additive of anti- American and anti-Semitic conspiracy theories.

Our journalism exposes the gap between rhetoric and reality – ideologically and organizationally – of violent jihadist groups. We do this through objective reporting that adheres to the highest standards of professional journalism. By covering violent extremism, we expose it for what it is.

Extremist groups have excelled at re-centering the news cycle on their violence. To counter this tactic, the BBG is pursuing several strategic goals in this space:

- Delegitimize extremism by reporting on and exposing the realities of extremist groups
- Make communities more resilient to extremism through engagement
- Promote diverse voices in the Muslim community otherwise overlooked in biased media environments

While other parts of the government directly support civil society, the BBG is uniquely positioned to elevate moderate voices – from the street to the elites. We cover local issues of concern, and provide constructive outlets for communities to discuss the issues that matter to them.

For example, the Middle East Broadcasting Networks' (MBN) "Raise Your Voice" campaign continues to successfully encourage citizens across the Middle East to speak out and be a part of the discussion about the fight against extremism. As a result, MBN has seen a large surge in digital traffic and on social media; in last four months over 590,000 votes have been cast on daily "Raise Your Voice" polls and MBN has 6.2 million followers on Facebook.

As part of the "Raise Your Voice" campaign, MBN launched *"Delusional Paradise"* in September, a weekly 30-minute documentary series comprised of firsthand accounts of families who have suffered at the hands of ISIL. This is precisely the kind of work the BBG should be doing: "*Delusional Paradise*" presents powerful firsthand and deeply moving accounts and interviews of families and communities that have suffered at the hands of ISIL. The program includes chilling interviews with families who have lost loved ones to ISIL recruitment, and compelling interviews with families victimized by ISIL attacks, including an interview with Jordanian pilot Muath al-Kasasbeh's family after he was burned to death by ISIL.

Internet Freedom

A third prominent challenge for us is the fundamental importance of information freedom. This is an enduring and central role for the BBG, from the Cold War to today.

Today, information freedom means the unfettered ability for people around the world to engage and connect with one another, to be informed, and ultimately to use that information to change their lives and the lives of their community for the better.

In 2002, the BBG created the Internet Anti-Censorship Program (or "IAC" program) to accomplish two major goals. The first is to support journalists, bloggers, civil society actors and activists to use the Internet safely and without fear of interference. The second is to empower world citizens to have access to modern, unrestricted communication channels and to allow them to communicate without fear of repressive censorship or surveillance.

Using funds provided by Congress for censorship circumvention programs, our International Broadcasting Bureau funds large scale proxy servers, such as Psiphon, and other means to defeat censorship. The BBG's investment and support of multiple circumvention technologies has helped to create a new generation of mobile apps that directly challenge and overcome the powerful government- enforced firewalls of Iran and China. Our web proxy servers allow more than one billion Internet sessions a day. Users from the Middle East, North Africa, Eurasia and East Asia are able to access news and information outside of their tightly controlled information markets.

Through our Open Technology Fund, we underwrite apps and programs for computers and mobile devices that help to encrypt communications and evade censorship. OTF's approach to identify and support next-generation internet freedom technologies has led to the development of first-of-its kind tools that encrypt text messages and mobile phone calls, detect mobile phone censorship and intrusion efforts, and allow transfer of data without use of the internet or mobile networks. Such efforts allow users facing constantly changing censorship methods to continue to communicate safely online.

We are seeing major success in this area. The BBG has internet freedom tools working in 200 languages. BBG/OTF's tools have supported nearly 1 trillion circumvention page views over the past year and the delivery of over 1 billion emails and newsletters delivered behind the Great Firewall of China every year. BBG currently provides the fastest Internet connectivity in Cuba, via satellite.

The success of our Internet Freedom work is at the core of our role as journalists and reflects our unique capabilities within the U.S. government. In the digital era, the freedom to speak and the freedom to listen remain essential. With the support of Congress, we aim to rapidly expand our presence and operations in this area.

Examples of Other Areas of Impact

The above cases are just a few examples of BBG's powerful impact in areas that are critical to U.S. foreign policy. But they are by far not the only instances. Some are more targeted but highly critical.

For example, in Nigeria, the eradication of polio was halted by rumors and misinformation about the safety of international vaccination programs. In response, Voice of America partnered with the Centers for Disease Control to carry out a multi-year campaign of reporting, Public Service Announcements, town hall meetings, and media trainings. In part due to our work to eliminate falsehoods surrounding the transmission of and vaccination against polio, Nigeria was just last month removed from the CDC's list of countries with endemic polio.

During protests and an attempted coup sparked by Burundian President Pierre Nkurunziza's decision to run for a third term, the government targeted independent media, forcibly closing down all privately-owned radio stations. However, VOA remains on the air via an owned-and-operated FM station in the capital, Bujumbura, which can be heard in most of the small country, as well as in refugee camps in Tanzania and the DRC. VOA is now one of the only available sources of news and information in Kirundi – the only language spoken by nearly all Burundians – as well as French and Swahili.

And, earlier this year, Somali President Hassan Sheikh Mohamoud contacted VOA's Somali Service to thank it for broadcasting a series on democratic constitution-making that he said was extremely valuable in his country's constitutional drafting conference in January 2014.

In conclusion, at a time of rapid geopolitical change and significant technological evolution, there are many new and unprecedented challenges in the global information space. In the face of these challenges, and with budgets that are far exceeded by those of our geostrategic competitors, the Broadcasting Board of Governors is having significant impact in some of the most difficult locations on earth. The Board views these successes as a foundation to build on and we hope that the Committee will remain cognizant of our growing success as it considers potential reforms.